WRITING & SELLING A NOVEL

P. 100
writes mass .

Other How To Books on Successful Writing

Copyright & Law for Writers
Creating a Twist in the Tale
Creative Writing
How to Be a Freelance Journalist
How to Master Business English
How to Publish a Book
How to Publish a Newsletter
How to Start Word Processing
How to Write a Press Release
How to Write a Report
How to Write an Assignment
How to Write an Essay
How to Write & Sell Computer Software
How to Write Business Letters
How to Write for Publication
How to Write for Television
How to Write Your Dissertation
Starting to Write
Writing a Nonfiction Book
Writing Reviews
Writing & Selling a Novel
Writing & Selling Short Stories

Other titles in preparation

The How To series now contains more than 150 titles in the following categories:

Business Basics
Family Reference
Jobs & Careers
Living & Working Abroad
Student Handbooks
Successful Writing

Please send for a free copy of the latest catalogue for full details (see back of cover for address).

SUCCESSFUL WRITING

WRITING & SELLING A NOVEL

How to craft your fiction for publication

Marina Oliver

IS THIS NECESSARY?

YES, IT HELPS WITH THE "CLIFF HANGERS"

How To Books

Cartoons by Mike Flanagan

British Library Cataloguing in Publication Data
A catalogue record for this book is available from the British Library.

First published in 1996 How To Books Ltd, Plymbridge House, Estover
Road, Plymouth PL6 7PZ, United Kingdom.

Note: The material contained in this book is set out in good faith for
general guidance and no liability can be accepted for loss or expense
incurred as a result of relying in particular circumstances on statements
made in the book. The law and regulations are complex and liable to change,
and readers should check the current position with the relevant authorities
before making personal arrangements.

Produced for How To Books by Deer Park Productions.
Typeset by PDQ Typesetting, Stoke-on-Trent, Staffs.
Printed and bound by The Cromwell Press Ltd, Broughton Gifford,
Melksham, Wiltshire.

Contents

LIST OF ILLUSTRATIONS

Acknowledgements

I would like to give heartfelt thanks to the writers and readers – the two ends of the writing business – and the essential intermediaries – the agents, editors, reviewers, librarians, and booksellers – all very busy people, who so generously and frankly answered my questions and gave freely of their knowledge and expertise.

There was a remarkable unanimity of views on many fundamental questions, whether from writers, agents, editors or readers. It will pay intending novelists to heed them. The authority of these people's varied experiences was invaluable, and their ways of expressing ideas much better than mine. I owe them much.

Where I have quoted directly it is because people have agreed that their comments can be attributed, and I have indicated names in brackets after the quotation. A list of names and positions is given in Appendix 1 at the end of the book. I am particularly grateful to Frances Hawkins and the members of the Ruislip Literary Society, and Jill Rundle and the Louth Writers' Circle who answered my questionnaire as groups, thereby increasing the range of answers.

A few people preferred anonymity, so I cannot extend public thanks to them, but they know how grateful I am for their answers.

Marina Oliver

Foreword

The old adage about writing being ninety-nine per cent perspiration and one per cent inspiration is certainly true. Many a talented writer has failed to achieve full potential because of a lack of perspiration. But having said that one also has to point out that the one per cent inspiration is essential. Without it you cannot begin. In over thirty years of editing I've observed that the inspiration is something you're born with – a mixture of observation and imagination and no amount of hard work can create the gift if it isn't there in the first place.

However, it is quite surprising how many people do have the talent to write, but for a wide variety of reasons manage to hide that talent, in some cases so well that it is hidden from even the most perceptive of editors. Sometimes the talent is obscured by sheer bad English – more of them than you would think! I once had a typescript submitted with an accompanying letter which said, 'dear sir I have writ a book'. Funny, yes, but also sad. There may well have been a talent there but a busy editor doesn't have the time or patience to wade through an ungrammatical, unpunctuated, mis-spelt typescript. Sometimes the writer is choosing the wrong medium for his or her talent – writing historicals when they should be writing thrillers, or fiction when biographies are their natural métier. The opening lines, paragraphs, chapters can be wrong, disguising the fact that halfway through the book *does* becomes exciting, but how many readers will persevere with a dull book in the hope it will improve? Characterisation, or the lack of it, is a common pitfall. I find I am often telling writers to go away and 'live with their characters' for a time, and then start again. All these things, and many more, can mean that a writer, who does have talent, may not make it to the printed page.

Writers *do* need all the help they can get in the way of professional expertise and general advice. Sometimes a friendly editor will spend

9

time on your particular problems, but a good beginning is to read as much as you can about general presentation, plotting, and crafting. The following pages may well pinpoint just what you need to know. Read, adapt, and apply. Then try again. And don't be discouraged. If you have the one percent inspiration, it will eventually win through!

Diane Pearson
Best-selling novelist, editor – Transworld Publisher,
President – The Romantic Novelists' Association

1
Taking Those First Vital Steps

'Some day I think I'll write a novel.' Many people express this wish but do no more. They don't have the burning desire to write which marks really committed writers. 'Everyone has a book in them' is a frequently stated belief. It may be true, but it's the getting it out that matters. This book is designed to help you put your novel on the page in the way that will give you the best chance of selling it. It's not easy, it can be hard work and often disappointing, and luck plays a critical part, but it *is* possible. With persistence, knowledge of your new world, and belief in yourself, you can succeed. The rewards, the delight in achievement, make all the effort worth while.

- 'Everyone has a certain amount of talent. Nurture it and keep practising. "Use it or lose it".' (Susan Sallis)

THE REASONS NOVELISTS WRITE

Why do you want to write a novel? Are your reasons the same as those of published novelists?

- 'To entertain.' (Ann Hulme, aka Ann Granger)

- 'To entertain the reader.' (Andrew Puckett)

- 'I want to tell a story, to entertain... like to create a time and place.' (Joan Hessayon)

- 'To provide leisure entertainment (and to give myself the pleasure of creation).' (Anne Melville)

- 'To tell a story, and for my own enjoyment, doing something I love.' (Marina Oliver)

11

- 'To entertain, to excite, to enlighten – but most of all to tell a good story.' (Frederick Nolan)

- 'Apart from the money!! To entertain and amuse, but most of all *to be read*.' (Anita Burgh)

- 'Almost always to tell a story in the way the story itself demands to be told. There are subsidiary aims too, such as: to pay the mortgage, to earn praise.' (Philip Pullman)

- 'To create a world looking from a new angle. A new perspective on the familiar.' (Matthew Kneale)

- 'To offer readers intelligent, and (I hope) entertaining and absorbing escapism from the endless stresses and strains of everyday life. Healthier than tranquilisers!' (Reay Tannahill)

BEING PROFESSIONAL

You want to write a novel, a long work of fiction which entertains, takes readers into an imaginary world. Perhaps you've written one and want to improve it. This book will:

- guide you through the basic techniques
- help you to avoid common pitfalls
- show you how best to present your work.

And 'remember that your first task is to entertain the reader.' (Sarah Molloy)

Behaving like a professional

Many people want to become novelists, but there is a crucial difference between most of them and you. You have made a start, shown a positive interest. You've already made a professional decision by reading this book, so keep on behaving like a professional. Tell yourself every day that you are not a scribbler or dabbler, but a proper writer.

- 'Never think of yourself as an amateur – once you put pen to paper you're a writer.' (Anita Burgh)

One definition of professionals is people who are paid for what they do. To get to that position they first have to show certain attitudes, apply standards which distinguish them from the amateur (in the sense of one who does not want to be paid, which does not imply worse in any way).

- (I look for) 'evidence that the author has a professional attitude.' (Carole Blake)

Checklist
Professionalism involves:

- **Attitudes** – Taking your work seriously.

- **Self-discipline** – You don't have a boss to supervise or tell you what to do.

- **Determination** – The will to succeed despite setbacks.

- **Time and energy** – You can always find some if you really want to.

- **Commitment** – Putting your writing as a top priority.

Having a professional attitude
As a professional writer you must display the qualities listed above, which are as vital to success as talent. One day, with them, you'll be paid too.

You are going to write a novel. Don't be apologetic or let anyone deter you. Other writers will understand your problems and anxieties so seek them out, talk with them, and most of all learn from them.

Working like a professional
Know what you are doing, creating a product for which there is a market. Authors, **agents** and **editors** create books, and the ultimate demand comes from readers through libraries and bookshops. But in a very real sense agents and editors are intermediary buyers of your product. You are the primary producer, they are the first buyers who process your work into the finished form, so you have to sell to them first. You need to know what they want, as they know what readers want, and be able to supply it on a regular basis. Start off with professional working practices.

- Organise your time and space to obtain the best possible working conditions.

- Be realistic in setting targets and evaluating work. (Tips on how to achieve these aims are given in the book *Starting to Write*, in this series.)

- Know your good and bad points, capitalise on the good ones and make allowances for the others.

- Don't be impatient, and don't give up at the first setback. Professionals persevere.

- 'If writing a novel seems like hard work, then you are in the wrong line of business. My first effort was comprehensively rubbished... I immediately sat down and started another.' (Joan Hessayon)

BEING METHODICAL

Targets
Time is valuable, especially when your writing must be fitted in with another job, and this applies to most writers at first. It isn't easy making a living from writing, and it can take several years to build up income. Writers cannot depend on writing income to begin with.

- 'Don't give up the day job until you've really made it.' (Barbara Levy)

If you are a compulsive writer, though, isn't it a wonderful feeling to think your hobby, if approached professionally, could bring in extra income?

How much time?
Don't think there isn't enough time after you've been to the office, or looked after children all day, or have lots of other interests. There is *always* time for writing, if that is your priority and if you give up other things.

To the question 'How much time per week did you spend writing before you were published?' I had the following replies, which show that dedication pays.

- 'a few hours' (Sara Banerji)
- 'eight to ten hours' (Anne Melville)

- 'two, three, four hours per evening five days a week.' (Frederick Nolan)
- 'fifteen hours' (Susan Sallis)
- 'five hours a day' (Joan Hessayon)
- 'I tried to spend at least ten hours.' (Andrew Puckett)
- 'I just made time' (Anita Burgh)
- 'Every spare moment including while vegetables boiled and babies napped. On bus and train journeys, you name it!' (Ann Hulme)

When?

Decide how much time each day or week you can devote to writing, and promise yourself you will spend that time sitting at your desk and doing the job.

Choose the time when you are most energetic. Many writers get up early to work. Most of the published writers said they did creative work in the mornings.

- 'Write every day.' (Philip Pullman)

This is the ideal, but if you genuinely can't, don't despair. Set weekly targets, so that you can catch up if some days you cannot write because of other claims. Longer stretches may suit you better than many brief ones.

- Keep a diary of your progress.

Thinking time

You need time for thinking too, for planning ahead or taking stock of what you've already done. You can plan the next chapter, work out the plot, get to know your characters. It's as important as getting the words onto paper. It's possible to do at all sorts of odd moments.

Your workplace

When and where you write will depend on circumstances. Try to be regular, to have your own desk always ready for use.

Typewritten scripts are essential

Your novel must be typed before it is sent to a publisher. Paying a typist is expensive, so it's worth learning to type and buying a word processor. You don't need an elaborate machine or expensive program, but buy the best printer you can afford, though remember that laser and inkjet are more expensive to run than dot-matrix.

The vast majority of professional writers now use word processors, though many begin with pen or pencil for their first draft. But beware. Sarah Broadhurst previews and reviews for *The Bookseller,* amongst other papers and magazines. She must hold the record for seeing the largest selection of new books, dealing with about 1,200 a year and says, 'I believe the word processor has seriously damaged the novel. Authors no longer have to type and retype, which is when a lot of dross was cut out, now it's just moved somewhere else and frequently shows.'

Organising your notes
Prepare a filing system to keep your notes, ideas and records where you can find them quickly.

Action points: making plans
1. Determine what time of day is best for your physical writing time.

2. Decide how much time you can devote to writing.

3. Calculate how much time during a typical day you could be thinking about writing while doing something else.

4. Devise an efficient working space, and set it up now.

NOVELS ARE EASIER TO PUBLISH THAN SHORT STORIES

Most fiction writers start with short stories because they take less time than novels. Markets for short stories are a few women's magazines, small specialist magazines and competitions. The supply of short stories is huge.

Fewer people attempt to write novels, yet over 8,000 titles (not all new ones) are published each year, by almost a hundred UK publishers or their individual imprints. Always check, since amalgamations and transfers of ownership are happening all the time. There is still competition, of course, but the chances of success are better with a greater demand and smaller supply. There is a list of publishers in Appendix 2, but it is not comprehensive.

THEY'LL TAKE SO MUCH TIME! A FALLACY

A novel could be 90,000 words long, and a typical short story 1,000 to 3,000 words. It seems a daunting task, but is it really such a big mountain? If you write a thousand words a day, let's say three pages, an hour's work, you can write a first draft of 90,000 words in three months. You will then have to spend time revising and redrafting, but you can write a novel in a year. When I was a full-time lecturer I often wrote 200,000 or more words a year.

Could you write and sell ninety short stories in a year, finding different plots, new characters and settings?

Action point
Keep a diary for a week or a month, and calculate how much you normally write per hour, then how long it will take you to write 100,000 words.

STUDYING THE MARKET

This is more important than many writers appreciate. It is not so that you can copy what is currently fashionable, but to know what is being published and what the trends are.

- 'Write what you want to write, from the heart, not what you believe to be fashionable. If you do the latter, by the time you've finished and the novel might be published trends will have moved on.' (Jane Morpeth)

- 'Please read what else is being published and understand what the publishing industry is looking for and why... It seems to me that the most successful authors are those who are exceptionally clued up about what is happening within the publishing industry and gear their work to those demands.' (Luigi Bonomi)

- (I often reject) 'writers who are completely out of touch with the market place and who don't themselves seem to read.' (Barbara Levy)

The books
There are different sorts of novels. They vary in length and in their emphasis on different aspects, but it's possible to group most of them into recognisable types.

The **genres** such as crime, romance, horror, science fiction, westerns and fantasy follow certain conventions and appeal to a restricted readership. So do the 'literary' novels, while 'mainstream' have a more popular, general appeal. You probably read several types yourself, and can say which genre a book fits into. It's likely you will want to write the sort of book you enjoy reading, so at first concentrate your market research on that type of book.

Action point
Make a list of your ten favourite books, say what type they are and why you enjoy reading them.

The publishers
Some publishers produce a wide variety of novels, others specialise.

Checklist
By making notes of:

- the titles of the books you study
- what sort they are
- what length they are
- what the style of writing is
- who publishes them
- which authors write them

you will begin to see some names repeated.

The bookshops
- (Authors) 'need to spend a lot of time in bookshops asking booksellers questions.' (Luigi Bonomi)

Action points: using bookshops for research
1. Spend a long time in a large bookshop. Shops stock the latest publications.

2. The few hardback novels will be the best-sellers and won't be much guide to you.

3. Look at paperback special categories such as crime, best-sellers, popular or twentieth century fiction.

4. Read the blurbs to see what the books are about, and what sort of people might be tempted to read them.

5. Make notes on which publishers are most often represented and which authors have several titles displayed.

The libraries
Librarians know a great deal about reading tastes, reviews and publishing trends. Talk to them.

Action points: using libraries

1. Read all you can of popular authors and the other, similar books their publishers do.

2. Consult specialist lists such as *The Guardian* annual list of the top hundred 'fast-sellers'.

3. Look at publishers' catalogues to see the range of books they publish.

4. Read the weekly magazine *The Bookseller*, available in most libraries, which has comprehensive review columns.

5. Look at the spring and autumn supplements of *The Bookseller* where publishers advertise forthcoming lists.

STUDYING THE CRAFT

Reading
Writers must read.

- 'Read and read and read and read and read. Read analytically, to see how the successful authors do it (and where they fail).' (Michael Legat)

Read novels and see why some are best-sellers. What do they have in common? Why are they popular?

Read books and articles about the craft of writing. Go to talks by writers. There are numerous day, weekend and longer courses for writers. You may wish to join a class or buy a writers' magazine.

The not-yet-published novelists I spoke to, who had all published other things, belong to groups and read books on writing. 'Most have at least one or two useful ideas – also they all encourage a positive idea.' (Zoë March)

Checklist: analysing what you read
Look at how the authors:

- use words
- use sentences and paragraphs
- introduce characters
- convey information about characters
- tell you what the conflict is, or the mystery
- describe the setting, the time or place, and technical details such as forensic or legal procedures
- use dialogue
- use description
- make characters vivid and memorable
- create tension
- use humour
- vary the pace
- make the most of important scenes
- arouse interest at the start
- maintain interest
- resolve conflicts or puzzles
- tie up loose ends
- finish satisfactorily.

Practising writing

Later in the book you will be given tips on how to do these things yourself. Writing is a craft and can be developed. We don't expect a painter to produce a masterpiece without first learning the techniques and trying them out. Look at every piece of writing you do as something you can learn from. If your submissions are rejected, that's hard, but most writers have experienced it. The successful ones are those who have learned from each lack of success (it isn't a failure, it just didn't win the prize) and go on to do better next time.

CASE STUDIES – MAKING A START

Sally makes a stab at it

Sally is 29 and has always loved reading. One day when her husband comes home to find her absorbed in a book, instead of collecting the twins from next door, he blows up.

'You waste so much time with your nose buried in a silly book. You can't get a job while the kids are little, but you ought to be able to write a book. You've got time to, and you read so many!'

Sally jumps up in excitement. 'Do you think I could? I've always dreamt of being a writer, but never had the guts to try. I'll dig my

old typewriter out tomorrow and do it!'
Sally spends the next few months writing away, all the time the twins are at school. When she's written the last page she parcels up the manuscript. She looks in the front of her latest library book for the publisher's address, copies it out and rushes out to post the parcel.

A month later the manuscript comes back with a typed rejection slip, on which someone has scribbled a note: 'Sorry, but we don't publish crime fiction.' Sally hasn't done her market research.

Don flounders in a glut of unpolished ideas

Don, made redundant at 40, starts his own business as a taxi driver. 'At first I'll spend a lot of time hanging around, so I can be scribbling a book. It must be easy. Just look at all the MPs who write crime books or thrillers,' he says to his wife.

For a few weeks he manages a page or two a day, then he runs out of ideas. He doesn't know much about police procedures, so he decides to turn his crime novel into a spy story. He can't have Russian spies now, but maybe Arabs will do. He reads an old guide book on Iran, but it isn't much help.

'We'll have to go on holiday to somewhere in the Middle East,' he suggests. 'We promised ourselves a good holiday with some of the redundancy cash.'

Three months later they have been on a Nile cruise, but have met very few Arabs apart from guides and touts. Don decides he can't write a spy story. He'll think of a good idea for science fiction.

Don hasn't thought out what he wants to do first.

Bridget does her preparation

Bridget was widowed in her early fifties, and wants something to occupy herself with.

'You were always good at composition at school,' her sister says. 'You had a couple of stories published, too, before the children were born. Why don't you write one of those short romances you see everywhere? I'm sure they're easy, you can read one in an afternoon.'

'You might,' Bridget says, 'but I never read them.'

'Oh, but surely anyone can write those!'

Bridget asks her librarian, who knows of a writers' group. Bridget goes to a meeting and meets several writers. They are friendly, eager to give advice, and recommend books and courses. One offers to read anything she writes and comment on it. Bridget begins to think in more detail of what sort of book she will write, and within six months is halfway through the first novel and going strong. She's done her research and it's paying off.

DISCUSSION POINTS

Some of these questions at the end of each chapter might form the basis of discussions or exercises at writers' group meetings, or you can consider them independently.

1. Novels can make one of the following the most important feature: the world in which the story is set; the problem to be solved; the relationships of the characters; major events of epic proportions. Find examples of each type.

2. Which type of novel do you want to write, and why? Is it for money or fame, because you have a story to tell, because you enjoy writing, or something else?

3. Do a brief summary (one page only) of a book you like, mentioning the aspects you feel are important, such as plot, characters, dialogue, the way it was written and so on. Then compare this with summaries of other novels.

2
Finding the Right Story

LOOKING FOR IDEAS EVERYWHERE

Which comes first, **plot** or **characters**? The answer to this often-asked question is either or neither. You need an idea for lift-off, and this can be a plot, a character, a setting, an incident, a theme, a title, a few words.

Where do you get ideas?

- 'There are always ideas – it's a question of which one.' (Susan Sallis)

- 'I try and think of lots of things – and hang on to the notions that don't seem stupid.' (Matthew Kneale)

- 'Anywhere and everywhere. I got a whole detective story from a few words overheard in a bus queue.' (Ann Hulme)

- 'I don't know. They come – some good, some not so good. You judge. You discard. You try. You learn.' (Frederick Nolan)

- 'A place, a person, a situation, a setting – something out of which other ideas come, and onto which I can graft more ideas.' (Marina Oliver)

- 'From living with and observing people.' (Andrew Puckett)

- 'Triggered off by news items or some personal event.' (Sara Banerji)

- 'Three-line paragraphs in newspapers... Anything will do which presents an interesting situation and prompts the question: "How did they get into this mess and how are they going to get out?"' (Anne Melville)

• My editor suggested that I write novels with some connection to gardening, and this has been the most helpful thing anyone said to me... I have plenty of ideas (but) not all the ideas are good ones... I choose a location and the place suggests a time and the time suggests a plot.' (Joan Hessayon)

Using ideas

All writers have too many ideas, the problem is knowing which make viable stories. You only need one to keep on working, it's the *way* you use ideas that's important.

You may have too few ideas because you are not yet used to recognising them for what they are or might be.

• 'I think when you've been writing for some time you recognise as story ideas thoughts which non-writers probably have just as frequently, but don't recognise because they don't use them.' (Philip Pullman)

Checklist

Find ideas through:

• people you know, see or read about
• places you know, go to, or read about
• major events such as war, terrorism, earthquakes
• historical events
• individual triumphs and tragedies
• phrases overheard
• diaries
• advertisements
• agony columns
• newspaper and magazine letter columns
• guide books
• myths, legends and fairy stories
• titles, first lines and quotations.

Ideas emerge from the subconscious, based on things we encounter. We then treat them consciously by bombarding them with information, playing with possibilities, planning how to use them and what we need to research about them.

Action point: Asking questions

Whenever you see, hear or read something which might be the germ of an idea, ask the following questions relating to it:

1. **Who** (are they, could they be, lives there)?
2. **What** (are they, do they do, is their nature)?
3. **How** (did it happen, did it get there, could it change)?
4. **When** (did it happen, did they meet, did they part)?
5. **Why** (did it happen then, there, and to them)?
6. **Where** (did it happen, and why there, and how)?
7. **What if** (any number of possibilities occur)?

AN EXAMPLE

Imagine a village with several houses around the green.

What are they? Let's suppose a vicarage, a general shop, an antiques shop, a pub, the home of a rich farmer, a weekender's cottage, cottages of farm labourers, a commuter to London, another to a nearby big town.

Who lives in each? There will be families, babies or teenage children, elderly relatives, *au pairs* or nannies, and they will have relatives and other visitors.

What jobs do they do? Not just the householder, but the rest of the family or the lodgers. Do they have hobbies or passionate interests or obsessions?

Given this wide selection of people, what are their backgrounds? Have they lived here long? What liaisons or quarrels might they have, amongst each other or outside?

What event, such as a newcomer arriving, or a proposal to build a new housing estate, or a sudden tragedy, might spark off a whole series of consequences?

If you haven't, by now, gleaned several ideas, go back and ask further questions, or devise different answers.

Keeping track of ideas
- 'Keep your eyes and ears open and *make notes!* You won't remember.' (Ann Hulme)

Write ideas down and file them. You will soon have far more than you will ever use, but just browsing through them can start the creative process off again.

PLOTTING

What is a plot?

You have had an idea, done some research, made lots of notes, and then perhaps you can't see the way forward or impose any sort of order on your creation. Don't worry. This is a normal part of the creative process.

Let it germinate, let the subconscious take over, and the mass of ideas and facts will begin to take on a shape, make patterns, and you have the basics of a plot. The important ideas and facts will float to the surface, begging to be used. Trust your instinct and take these to work on. Your novel will start to become more real, a concrete idea instead of a hazy mass of unconnected snippets.

Theme

Theme is not the same as plot, it's the impulse behind the plot. It's often an abstract notion like jealousy, revenge, or ambition.

A story is not necessarily a plot, though we tend to use the words interchangeably. A story can be a series of events, rather like diary entries. A plot is more.

This happened because

A plot is a series of cause and effect events told in a dramatic way. The actions described have consequences. As the author you are in control in that you are deciding what events are important and showing them in a particular way.

Being original

The events you are relating must be strong, realistic and believable, but different and original.

Don't worry if you cannot find a plot which seems original. It's been said there are only so many plots, though the precise number varies. It's the treatment that matters. Plots are like a Lego board – the same limited variety of shapes and colours which can be built up into hundreds of different combinations. If you gave ten people the same basic idea, situation and set of characters you would have ten different plots.

Being believable

Even in fantasy you need to make readers suspend disbelief.

• 'I do like a book to catch my imagination somehow, with that magical combination of character and narrative that makes me care what happens even while I know it is fiction.' (Mary Brackley)

Readers know it's unreal, but for the time they are reading they want to believe, and it's up to you to convince them by making your characters real, the plots logical, and the resolutions of crises apparently inevitable. Don't make your characters do impossible things, and remember it's lazy plotting and breaks your implied contract with the reader to get out of difficulties with unforeseeable coincidences, or bringing on the *deus ex machina*, the god who arrives to sort out the mess made by mere mortals.

Devising a plot
Set up the initial situation, the relationships, obsessions and the conflicts. Now, and throughout the book, ask 'What happens next?' You could go off in many directions, but aim to have reasonable, believable developments, yet not the boringly obvious. You want to surprise readers while convincing them that your plot is right and inevitable.

Bring in complications, increase the conflict and intensity, prevent your characters from reaching their objectives too easily. Towards the climax develop the main crisis which is then confronted, have the showdown and get it resolved satisfyingly.

When characters determine plot
At this stage you also need characters who will be the means of acting out the plot. If you have the right people in the right situations they will to some extent determine the plot through the development, or revelation, or interactions of characters. All the time ask 'What if this happens?' and what different characters would do in particular situations.

You can start with some characters and a situation and see where it leads you, since a complicated story will twist and turn in ways which surprise the author too.

- 'I don't plot, I just "go with it".' (Anita Burgh)

Starting with the end
You can alternatively start at the end and plan how to get there. Many, though not all, crime novels start with the ending.

Play on the emotions of readers, make them share the emotions of the characters, but remember that emotion without action is not a plot.

The shape of a plot

A plot progresses through a series of peaks and troughs, high and low points, crises and reflection. There will be lots of small crises, building towards the major one.

You are likely to have subplots which need to be woven in, like a plait. They can be brief, soon resolved, or almost as long as the main plot. They can involve the main characters or minor ones, or both. They need developments, crises and resolutions in the same way as the main plot.

Pre-planning

It is advisable for beginners to draw up an outline of what is likely to happen, to save going too far off track. It could cause months of rewriting if you don't decide beforehand whether your plot can work, whether the time-scale fits in, whether you can get your characters in the right places when you need them there.

If you have only a sketchy plan, though, don't worry. Writers differ enormously in how they work, including how much they plan ahead. Many have little or no idea of what will come next. Many say that when they start they know where they are going, but not the route by which they get there. Others write vast outlines.

- 'I start with a full synopsis (forty single-spaced pages of it). Ideas seem to flow more freely in a synopsis, when there are no stylistic problems to slow them down. Though I may depart from the framework when I begin writing, having a proper framework means that I never stray too far.' (Reay Tannahill)

Try to express the basic plot in one sentence.

DOING RESEARCH

Why is this necessary?

'Write what you know.' It would be very restricting if we all wrote only about our personal knowledge and experience. Most of us have limited experience, but we have imagination. Without this we would have no science fiction, fantasy, historicals, and very few crime books. 'Write what you already know about or can research' is better advice.

Some research is necessary for most novels. You won't know all the details you need, and if you don't know them you won't convince the reader. Many best-sellers are based on vast amounts of research and insider information which the novelist gleans and then portrays dramatically. But beware of dragging in facts which are not relevant to the story and don't carry it forward in some way.

Readers said that they particular enjoyed novels which:

- 'have information about the running of a business and work' (Valerie Bennett)

- 'are set in a different part of the country/world/age.' (Nancy Brazier)

Checklist: What you already know
- What jobs have you done?
- What hobbies and interests do you have?
- What countries have you been to?
- Which parts of the UK do you know best?

Where to do it
You don't often need to consult primary sources such as documents and letters in dusty archives, since these have usually been written about by scholars trained to read Latin or archaic handwriting. Read their articles or books.

It does help, though, to see places for yourself, or visit museums and history theme parks, or read contemporary newspaper accounts. You can explore specialist libraries, look at detailed maps, talk to experts, ask public and private organisations for information.

When to do it
Preliminary research will be needed to help organise your plot and check that it is feasible. It will often provide ideas for characters or incidents to use.

- I research extensively – more than I will ever need – because everything I read feeds my ideas for plot development and incident, especially incident.' (Joan Hessayon)

Some details will have to be checked as you come across the need for them while you write. During later revision you may need to check or confirm facts.

Note the sources of facts you collect, in case you need to go back for more details, or have to provide proof.

Action points

Make lists, with addresses and telephone numbers, of:

1. Libraries in your area, particularly big or special ones, with, if possible, names of contacts – people you know or have met or spoken to during earlier research. It is easier to ask for a specific person, and makes a good impression that you remember them.

2. Museums and theme parks in your area.

3. People you know or have been told about who have any expert knowledge. Most experts are only too happy to answer questions or talk about their speciality.

Being methodical

Arrange your notes for easy reference. Use folders, record cards, or computer files, whichever is most convenient.

CASE STUDIES: GETTING DOWN TO BASICS

Sally skimps the work

Sally is disappointed that her first script came back. She soon cheers up when she decides to write a historical romance. 'All I have to do is describe long dresses and have men in doublets and hose, and riding horses,' she says.

She has read that editors prefer to see just the first three chapters, and this will save her work if they reject it again. She dashes off fifty pages and sends it to a different publisher. It comes back, but on the rejection slip the editor has written, 'Your writing is vivid and lively, but you need to get the historical details right.'

Sally is furious. 'How do they expect me to be an expert! I haven't got time for all that research.'

Sally isn't doing her job properly.

Don accepts he needs to plan ahead

Don is sorting through his pile of manuscripts, none of them more than about thirty pages long.

'I just can't follow through on the first ideas,' he complains.

'Perhaps you need to plan it in detail first,' his daughter suggests. 'There's a guy at school whose mother writes crime novels. She talked to us once, and she starts at the end, she knows who did the murder, and works back putting the clues in place before she begins to write.'

'Hmm.' Don doesn't want to feel that his daughter is telling him how to do it, but he thinks hard about what she says, and the next day begins to work out another crime novel idea. It does seem easier this way, and soon he has a pile of notes and is ready to start again.

Bridget has no plot

Bridget has written a hundred pages before she plucks up courage to show her work to Jane, the writer friend who has offered to read it for her. 'What do you think?'

'You write well, but you don't have enough plot.'

'I have lots of things happening,' Bridget says, hurt.

'Yes, but it's just a string of dates when the man takes the girl out to restaurants, or sailing, or whatever, and lots of petty squabbles about minor things. You must give them some really big problem that divides them, and then make each incident lead into the next, and every quarrel have some result. It doesn't work properly when they just storm away and then make it up the next day.'

Bridget nods slowly. 'I see. I'll have to start all over again, and I thought it was going well.'

Bridget begins to think what plot really means.

DISCUSSION POINTS

1. Write down as many themes as you can think of, and under each one make notes of the sort of plots they inspire.

2. Write down a detailed list of everything you did today, read, heard on radio, watched on TV, and the people you saw. Try to find an idea from each item or person which might become an incident in a novel.

3. Think of some different settings, such as Roman Britain, present-day Australia, an oil company, a spaceship voyage, and make lists of the sort of research you might have to do for each and how you would set about it.

3
Creating the Right Characters

CHOOSING YOUR CAST WITH CARE

I use the word cast deliberately, since your characters are actors in a drama. See them this way, in scenes on a stage. It helps to bring them alive for you, and therefore helps you to make them real for your readers. Visualise the action as it takes place. Most writers find this works.

- 'I find it very useful (particularly in thrillers or action stories) to draft in dialogue only, no descriptions, no scene-setting. Once the words are there, it's much easier to see where the exposition should be.' (Frederick Nolan)

Characters must be right for your novel. They can provide ideas for the plot, for incidents and twists.

- 'The action arises from the people in the story reacting in character to the situation in which they find themselves.' (Ann Hulme)

Deciding how many characters

Create as few as you can get away with. P. G. Wodehouse said one big one was worth two small ones. There will be:

(a) Some who are essential in order to do certain things; these vary from the main characters to the unseen train driver without whom they could not move around.

(b) Real people have family, friends, neighbours and colleagues. They give your main characters a background with all the relationships and complications involved, even if they don't feature directly in the story.

(c) Others round out the lives or demonstrate character traits of the main characters, even if off-stage. This could be a bedridden old lady the heroine visits, which can show her compassion or helpfulness.

Making them know their places

The scale of importance varies. In category romances very few characters appear apart from the hero and heroine. In most crime novels several characters have to be of similar importance to provide a believable list of suspects.

Checklist

On your list you are likely to have:

- Two at the top: the hero and heroine, the sleuths, the opposing army commanders. These are the main **protagonists**.

- Perhaps several biggish ones who are on stage a lot, powerful enough to influence events and about whom readers *care*. Caring is not liking. Readers care about a character when they want him to receive his just deserts, be this reward or punishment. If readers are indifferent to a **major character** the writer has not succeeded.

- Some **minor characters** who play important parts, but don't appear very much.

- And the **walk-ons** like waiters and postmen who are essential in the tasks they perform, but only scenery.

Action points

Get organised:

1. Take a novel you know well and list all the characters in order of importance, labelled protagonists, major, minor and walk-ons. Could any of them be dispensed with totally, or their role be given to another character?

2. Do the same with your own casts of characters.

FLESHING OUT CHARACTERS

Having a variety

In most plots you need people of different sexes, ages, appearances, occupations and dispositions. This makes the situation more natural and interesting.

Two examples of different characters – Plot out of characters

	Kate	Ann
Name	Kate	Ann
Age	25	21
Physical appearance	tall, slim, strong features, long red hair, green eyes	medium height, short wavy brown hair, brown eyes, slightly plump, pretty
Occupation	freelance artist	secretary to sales manager of local factory
Family background	Father a diplomat, retired; mother remarried to a French count ten years ago; older brother, policeman	Father a bank manager; mother dead five years ago; younger sister, 16, at school
Schooling	expelled from three boarding schools	local comprehensive, top of class, prefect
Disposition	extrovert	confident but quiet and dreamy
Where lives now	flat in London	home, country town
With whom	two girls and two men sharing	father and sister
Clothes liked	offbeat, latest fashion	good classics, has a few disasters with experiments
Hobbies/interests/ likes/dislikes	powerful motorbike; travel to exotic places; likes jazz, indifferent to food, hates cats	cooking, music, environmental and 'green' issues; enjoys foreign foods, country and western, dislikes arguments
Virtues	casually kind, fierce against injustice	well organised, competent, soft-hearted
Faults	always short of cash, quick-tempered	critical of sister, obstinate
Previous romantic history	two lovers, brief affairs which she ended	engaged at 19 to salesman at work, he jilted her for her best friend

Fig. 1. Two character profiles.

- 'Ideally every character should have an individual voice (as people do in life) – particular turns of speech, favourite phrases, a tendency to be slangy or pedantic.' (Reay Tannahill)

Readers often like to read about people from similar groups to their own, but they also want characters to be intriguing, different from themselves.

In certain stories characters need someone in whom they can confide or with whom they can discuss or share information. Most detectives have a sidekick, most heroines a best friend. Make these characters interesting in themselves, active in the story. Give them other functions.

Getting to know them
Many writers, though not all, compile lists of their characters' physical and other attributes before they start.

- 'Write a potted biography for each one.' (Andrew Puckett)

This helps writers to remember what characters look like, but also to know how they might react to various situations. They are notes for guidance, however, and are not necessarily used in the book. As the book progresses, too, other attributes are likely to be added to the basic list.

Checklist: Building a character profile
Answer these twenty questions about your main protagonists and major characters. Can you think of other questions?

- name
- age and date of birth
- physical appearance
- family background
- where brought up
- schooling
- where lives now
- with whom
- first job
- other jobs
- present occupation
- disposition
- clothes liked/disliked
- hobbies/interests

- other likes/dislikes (*eg* food, music, books, animals)
- virtues
- faults
- ambitions
- secrets
- romantic history.

Action points: Characters and plots

1. Keep this outline ready and refer to it when you are creating new characters.

2. Look at the diagram in Figure 1 listing the characteristics of two different girls, and try to see what kinds of conflicts might develop, what plots might be possible using them.

Names are critical

Names do far more than identify characters. Some authors cannot begin until they have named their cast. Names can tell you a lot.

- Family names can indicate social inheritance (Saddler or Fitzroy) or ethnic background (O'Leary or Patel).

- First names often indicate age if associated with film stars (Marilyn or Wayne) or an event or passing fashion (Jubilee or the Puritan names such as Temperance).

- Characters may be named after a relative or historical personage, which can say something about their parents, as do names which are either very popular or unusual.

- Hard vowel sounds indicate curtness, soft ones gentleness.

- Make sure your characters are easily differentiated by having some names short, some long, and of different rhythms or patterns, such as the stress on first or last syllable.

- Don't have the same initial letter for similar characters unless it's important to the plot.

- If your story takes place in a real town, now or in the past, with a solicitor called Harvey Anstruther, make sure there isn't such a real person. Check telephone, commercial, street and professional directories.

- Characters may be called something different by other characters. Mr Brown can be David, darling, daddy, grandpa, sir, or you bastard. The narrator should always refer to him by the same name, introduce him by that one, and make it obvious who is calling him by what variation.

Make lists of names, and the characteristics you might associate with each. Then ask deeper questions, give the characters a twist, and find less obvious attributes.

Action points: Keeping track

There are many ways to help you remember your characters, apart from the profile you have compiled.

1. Cut photographs from magazines and newspapers of people who resemble your characters, and keep them visible.

2. List the main physical and other details alongside for reference. If you have room put the profiles there too.

3. Draw up family trees with dates of birth, marriage and death.

4. Draw diagrams of their houses and neighbourhoods, decorate and people them.

5. Avoid the trap of putting all this into your novel. Like most other research it's for guidance, helps you to be accurate, propping up what's visible but not intruding. Only mention a fact when it's relevant.

6. Keep away from stereotypes, apart from walk-ons who don't want to be noticeable by having any peculiarity.

7. Make your characters complex, with many different facets while still being recognisable. You could exaggerate something, or give them an obsession, to make them more interesting.

8. If a character is going to behave in an especially odd manner, though, give clues early on, don't spring it on the unsuspecting reader.

9. Start collecting a rogues' gallery of photos to use.

Believing in your characters

They must be absolutely real to you, or you won't make readers believe in them. Live with them, get inside them, know them as well as you possibly can. We all give something of ourselves when we write fiction, and though we might never commit murder we have to be able to know what it feels like to want to do it. We are complex people with good and bad points, our characters must be too.

Creating sympathy for them

A character is 'sympathetic' when the reader believes in him, likes him, can imagine being him, approves his aims, wants him to achieve them. Readers approve of protagonists who are admirable, dependable, generous. They loathe bullying or ruthless greed, though they may be fascinated by such characters and enjoy the *frisson* of meeting them.

● 'You have to start with a personality that attracts. The reader has to identify. Heroes can't be wimpish.' (Joan Hessayon)

● 'Make your main characters your friends – if you love them there is more chance of your readers doing the same.' (Anita Burgh)

If your protagonist has only unpleasant or despicable traits most readers won't identify with him, although they might understand him. If a protagonist is a victim he must still be strong, it shouldn't be his own fault, and he mustn't give up. His sacrifices must be worth while.

I asked some not-yet-published novelists what they found most difficult. 'Characterisation' (Diana Atkinson) was a typical reply. It must be worked on.

Agents and editors look for:

● 'Characters.' (Caroline Sheldon)
● 'Good characters.' (Jane Morpeth)
● 'Good characterisation.' (Bob Tanner)
● 'Carefully developed characters.' (Laura Longrigg)
● 'Involvement with the characters.' (Elizabeth Johnson)
● 'Getting involved with the characters, caring about them.' (Dorothy Lumley)
● 'Original characters.' (Beverley Cousins)
● 'Being interested in the characters, caring what happens to them, and how.' (Deborah Smith)

- 'Good characterisation.' (Barbara Boote).

  Readers want:

- 'I must care about the characters.' (Jûdy Phillips)
- 'Interesting and believable characters.' (Joan Beard)
- 'Some depth to characters.' (Valerie Bennett).

Making your characters grow

Many changes occur as time passes, marriage and children, different houses and jobs, but we also change in response to experiences. Your characters must too. They must be different at the end of the story, because of the conflict and its resolution, and this difference can be an improvement or not. It must be believable, however. Often the apparent change is in effect a discovery, a stripping away of a surface disguise to the real character beneath.

Showing your characters

You need to transfer your character profiles into your novel without being obvious. You cannot simply list the character's qualities in a piece of description. This would be boring, difficult for the reader to absorb, and unsubtle. In the same way as you know real people from what they are and do, you can portray your characters indirectly.

Checklist

Show characters by:

- what they do now
- what they have done in the past
- how they do things
- why they do things
- how other people see them
- how other people talk about them
- how other people behave towards them
- their beliefs, habits, hobbies, interests, tastes, preferences
- what they say and how they say it.

Letting characters take over

Cardboard, two-dimensional characters, are puppets which the author pushes around. If you have created truly believable people you may find that your plans for them aren't compatible with how they are. Then you need to adjust either the character or the plot.

One story may work with a certain character, not with others. Authors who create characters and follow where they lead know this, and their books don't depend a great deal on plot. Authors who rely too much on a pre-ordained plot may find their characters wooden and incredible. Most novels are a balance.

- 'I have to be sure that both plot and characters will be strong enough to stand up to what I want of them, and it's surprising how many apparently promising ideas turn out to be far too slight.' (Reay Tannahill)

Action point
Look at some books you've read recently. Which are character-led, which plot-led, which balanced?

WORKING OUT RELATIONSHIPS AND CONFLICTS

Keeping the heroes on-stage
The protagonists, the most important characters, should be on stage as often as possible.

- They should be given most to do, should be active and make things happen, not simply react to events.

- They must solve the mystery, tackle the villain, perform the heroic tasks.

- They should not be there performing a minor role while a subsidiary character takes the limelight or does something heroic which your main character could have done.

- Their aims must be laudable.

- They must face and overcome difficulties.

- They must be strong though vulnerable.

- Some imperfections can be attractive, and even murder by a hero could be acceptable in a good cause, such as destroying a terrorist.

- 'One hundred per cent nice characters are very difficult to bring to life. Even the most romantic heroes and heroines need a few human failings.' (Reay Tannahill)

Provide conflict

Whatever the cause of conflict, readers must care about the result. What's at stake has to be important, to matter greatly. The protagonists or opposing sides have different aims which cannot both be achieved, although the reader may want both to be achieved. Then a satisfactory solution or compromise has to be found. There can also be inner conflict when one character has contradictory objectives.

Action point

Make a list of as many causes of conflict as you can think of, from books you have read or your imagination.

CASE STUDIES: GETTING ACQUAINTED

Sally chooses badly

Sally has read some books about writing, and understands that her characters have to alter somehow during their experiences. She begins to write a story about an unpleasant, selfish girl who would, because of seeing a big plane crash and helping a couple of survivors, change into a caring, happy person everyone loves.

'But she's so very horrid I don't enjoy writing about her,' she tells her husband.

'If you don't like her, will anyone else?'

'So I have to start again. Can I make her nicer?'

'Wouldn't it be better to forget her, and have a quite different sort of person?'

'I suppose so. At least I can use her in some book, as a villain, a baddie,' Sally says, cheering up.

Don tries to think of everything

Don has read that it is sensible to make a list of all the characteristics of every person in his novel. He finds he enjoys creating imaginary people, getting them different in as many ways as possible. His wife reads the first chapter.

'Why does the shop assistant have his arm in a sling, and a limp?' she asks. 'Is it explained later?'

'No,' Don says. 'He doesn't come in again.'

'A pity. I thought he was going to be exciting.'

'Do you like my descriptions of the two policemen?'

'It's a lot to remember all at once. I get Jack muddled with Jock, except that Jack likes grapefruit for breakfast and Jock porridge. I suppose that's because he's Scottish. And hardly anything happens apart from the telephone call to the station about the body they've found.'

Don has described too much, too early, and selected confusing names. He has also delayed the action, and aroused unjustified expectations with his limping shop assistant.

Bridget sorts it out

Bridget thinks hard about Jane's advice on plotting. She has made lots of notes about her characters. The early deaths of her heroine's parents have made the girl wary of depending on anyone else, determined to succeed alone. How might this give conflict with the hero? She has an idea. Instead of making him a loner, too, he could be the eldest child of a father who was rarely home, and a mother who left her children to be looked after by nannies or *au pairs*. He was used to looking after his brother and three sisters, and he wants to organise the heroine too.

Bridget has found one cause of conflict out of the characters themselves, their backgrounds. They will both have to compromise if it is to become a satisfying romance.

DISCUSSION POINTS

1. If you have decided what sort of novel to write, make a list of possible characters and how you might use them.

2. Take a well-known fictional character like Jane Eyre or Oliver Twist, put them in a new age and place and situation, and work out how they might behave and with what consequences. What effects might a different historical and social background have on their characters?

3. Take three characters, let's say a wimpish young man, a bossy young woman, and a middle-aged mother of three boys. They see a nasty fight begin between two young teenage lads, and one boy pulls a knife. How would each react? Write the scene showing what they might do and say.

4
Getting Ready to Start

You have an idea, a plot and some characters. You will have lots of notes, and maybe a rough outline of what you mean to do. There are several more decisions to make before you can begin to set the novel down in narrative form.

CHOOSING THE RIGHT TITLE

This doesn't have to be chosen first, but titles often come during the planning stage. Consider ideas now, since a title often expresses the main theme of the novel.

Sometimes titles only come when the book is finished. A phrase, or incident, or character can give an idea. Don't worry if you can't think of the ideal title now, but work hard to find a good one before you send your manuscript out.

Titles are important
Some editors say a good title helps catch their attention.

- 'A good title is one of the most important parts of a novel.' (Luigi Bonomi)

A sparkling or intriguing title helps to sell a book, according to booksellers. Agents were not so positive, but at this stage titles can be changed, and frequently are. Publishers may have their own preferences, or they may have published a book with a similar title and don't want to confuse readers. Librarians were divided about whether titles attracted readers, and most readers said they went mainly for familiar authors rather than titles, though titles might put them off reading a book.

- 'I think I could be discouraged.' (Hanna Bridgeman)
- 'Can be off-putting.' (Ruislip Literary Society)

Although titles appear less significant to readers, they still matter. Readers only see what has been published. Your first readers are agents and editors, who will see your originality and writing talent.

Titles must be appropriate

Ideally titles are short, two or three words, since these fit better onto a book jacket and spine. Words of two and three syllables, with a rhythm, work best.

They should convey something about the *type* of book. Look at how many crime books use the words murder, death, or mystery; and romances love, bride, or heart. Historicals try to indicate the period, and recent blockbusters have used the themes as one-word titles.

Finding titles

Many titles are straightforward descriptions, while others come from puns, or plays on words or common phrases. Some use alliteration. Many are quotations or phrases from poems, Shakespeare or the Bible.

Keep in mind your intended reader and choose something which they will understand and appreciate.

Action points: finding titles

1. Think up some alternative titles for famous books, or ones you have read recently.

2. Make lists of titles you might one day use.

USING THE RIGHT VIEWPOINTS

The choice you make now will have important implications for how you tell the story.

Choosing the most effective viewpoint

Viewpoint is the manner in which the story is told, through whose eyes. It's as if the scene is being told by one of the characters. When you are reading a book notice how an author keeps the main interest of a scene or chapter with one person, and shows as if from inside her how she feels, and how she sees the actions and emotions of others.

Different stories require different approaches, and no one method is best for every story or every author. Decide which characters, one or more, can best tell the story.

There are technical terms describing the options, such as

omniscient. This means that the narrator sees everything from some lofty outside standpoint, entering into each character's mind in turn, but having an overall view separate from them all. Many Victorian novels were written like this. It keeps the reader at a distance from the characters, not allowing them to identify with any one for very long, and is little used today.

There are two main viewpoint techniques used today, **first** or **third** person, and both usually told in **past tense**.

First person problems

The first person (I) narrator, where one character tells the story as if she is writing it, is sometimes essential, often used, and can be effective in conveying intense emotion, but there are difficulties.

* You need devices to have her present when important things happen, or being told of them in an interesting way. She needs valid reasons for obtaining the information.

* The fact that she is telling the story means she survived threats or danger, so an element of suspense is lost.

* She can only tell what she sees and interprets of other people's actions, feelings and emotions, or what they tell her, and this may not be the full truth.

* It is sometimes difficult to avoid the impression of being self-absorbed, with too many 'I's, or boring or boastful, especially if the narrator is the heroine and has to describe her own brave or meritorious actions.

Third person techniques

A third person narrator can tell the story mainly through one person's eyes.

* This will tend to be male or female depending on the likely readership.

* It will usually be the main protagonist.

* The author can switch viewpoint to scenes when the main character is absent, or get inside other characters and show their emotions.

- It is the most used today, it's the simplest method and usually best to begin with, until you have more experience.

How many viewpoints?

If you choose the third person viewpoint you can use it in various ways, but bear the following points in mind.

- Keep the viewpoint characters to a minimum, because switching demands special skills, and too many viewpoints can be confusing and diffuse attention and sympathy.

- Normally use the main characters, though it can be effective, very occasionally, to show a scene through the eyes of a character uninvolved in that specific conflict.

- It's best, at least to start with, to keep to the same viewpoint within one chapter.

- In long chapters broken up into several distinct scenes keep one viewpoint per scene. Switching too frequently confuses the readers.

Action points: Looking at viewpoints

1. Read a book written from the first person viewpoint, and see where the author has constructed devices such as a letter, or eavesdropping, or a report from someone else to allow the narrator access to information.

2. Read another book where several third person viewpoints are used, and make a list of who narrates, and when the changes are made. Is a pattern emerging?

ESTABLISHING YOUR VOICE

Our physical speaking voices differ from those of others. We write more formally than we talk, choosing different words and sentence constructions. We use gestures when talking, and other aids like punctuation when writing. We both talk and write differently depending on our audience. When talking, if we are astute we detect lack of comprehension in our audience and adjust what we say accordingly. We cannot do this when writing so have to be aware of likely problems and forestall them.

All these different ways of communicating are our own very special styles, using our individual voice. Experts can often identify an author or composer from a small fragment of writing or musical score. Voices with special qualities of freshness, humour, clarity or perceptiveness will be recognised and valued.

Don't attempt to copy anyone else's style. You won't do it consistently or with conviction, and falsity seems to be magnified and becomes glaringly out of place.

GETTING THE BEGINNING RIGHT

Now you can start writing the first chapter, which is perhaps the most important one you have to do. The first few sentences can make or break a novel.

The narrative hook

A title and **jacket**, which most librarians thought very important, may tempt readers to pick your book from the shelves. One librarian said a bad cover design wouldn't prevent a reader taking a book by an author she knew, and in any case most books were displayed with only the spine showing. However, a librarian pointed out: 'Attractive artwork will encourage us to use it in displays.'

And books displayed, as well as those on the returns trolley, are often the first chosen by many readers.

Potential readers may look at the **blurb**, which both readers and librarians rated as more important than the title, but in most cases they then turn to page one. This is where you must tempt them to continue and not replace the book on the shelf. You need to work especially hard to get the first few paragraphs as perfect as possible.

Action point

Read these two openings, and say which you prefer and why. Which would you be most likely to read further?

Evergreen

Angela Jones sighed as she looked out of the staffroom window. It was raining cats and dogs, and she'd forgotten her umbrella again. She would be drenched when she reached home, for it was a good half-hour's walk.

Angela's home was a small terraced house in Pitsfield, a suburb of Shelcaster. It had once been a mining village, and her father still worked in the last remaining coalmine in the area. His father and grandfather had also worked there, as had her mother's father and brothers.

Her parents had been determined to let Angela take every chance that came her way, and had denied themselves small luxuries so that she could stay on at school to take her A-levels, and then go to the local university. It would have been too expensive for her to go anywhere else, they'd said, and besides, they wanted their ewe-lamb to stay at home with them.

So Angela had worked hard, taken a lower second in English, and done her teacher training. She'd been fortunate to find a job in Lodge Road First School, so near to home, but so far when it was raining and there were no buses going cross-country.

The Tinderbox

Annie swore vividly as she stepped into a deep puddle. And to think that only a week ago she'd been praying for rain. Things changed! She leaned forward to look at the muddy splashes on her new tights, then gasped as her elbows were seized by hard, relentless fingers.

'You're a menace even without an umbrella!' a deep masculine voice said angrily.

Annie struggled to free herself and her purse slipped from under her arm. 'You! Now look what you've done. What on earth are you doing here anyway? I thought you'd gone to Syria. And let me go, you're hurting.'

She struggled, but was dragged ruthlessly into the shelter of a doorway. Her umbrella was taken from her hands, shaken viciously then furled, and a moment later her purse, streaming muddy water, was thrust at her.

'You told Sara we were going to be married. Why?'

Annie took a deep breath. 'I – I – well, I meant it for the best,' she eventually stammered. 'I thought it was a good idea.'

He laughed, unamused. 'You've never had a good idea in your life. You're a walking disaster zone, and I'm going to make damned sure you never again interfere in my life!'

Comparison of the sample openings
Titles
1. *Evergreen* sounds dull and old-fashioned.

2. *The Tinderbox* gives more indication of excitement.

Action
1. Almost none, just description and thoughts.

2. Immediate physical and verbal conflict.

Style
1. Many clichés (raining cats and dogs, take every chance that came her way, denied themselves small luxuries, ewe-lamb), the language is gentle, and only the first paragraph is from Angela's viewpoint. The rest is exposition.

2. From Annie's viewpoint, and contains expressive words.

Character
1. Angela is dependent on her family, not very clever if she only obtained a lower-second degree after working hard, and somewhat complaining as she sighs about the rain.

2. Annie has strong emotions, can perhaps laugh at herself (Things changed!), gets into scrapes, and doesn't think ahead. Which girl is the more interesting?

Future promise
1. Almost no questions to ask about Angela. No idea what sort of story it might be. No conflict looming.

2. With Annie, though, we want to know who the man is, why she thought he was in Syria, who Sara is, and why Annie told her she was getting married when she wasn't, and how he is going to stop her from further interference. There's plenty of conflict promised.

Making it active
The most effective beginning is to get right into the action. You can begin with a description of a setting or a character, but this is static, less easy to do, and can therefore be boring. It's not advisable until you have acquired a lot of skill.

Action implies a scene, with characters. They are doing something, preferably caught in the middle, bang, not about to begin with a lot of build-up and explanation. If possible make it just before a major event or confrontation. You can give the necessary background information later on, explain who they are and what is happening. If you have enticed readers to turn over the first page in order to find this out you are half-way to persuading them to read the whole book. And always remember that your first reader is the editor who may buy your book.

Readers' views

Readers said it was important that books:

- 'gain my interest in the first few pages.' (Jo Crocker)

- have 'good style and story.' (Sylvia Parker)

- have a 'style of writing which you know from the first page – the book grabs you or not.' (Molly Frearson)

- and, when choosing 'I look at the first part.' (Jill Rundle)

- 'I like to get into it quickly.' (Judy Phillips)

    Agents said the same. Scripts stood out with:

- 'the ability to tell a story which hooks the reader from the first page.' (Sarah Molloy)

- and 'an urge to read on after the first few pages.' (Bob Tanner)

    Editors tell the same story:

- 'a powerful opening chapter.' (Luigi Bonomi)

Checklist

The functions of the first few pages are:

- to attract the reader's interest
- to indicate the type of book
- to show the mood and style of the writing
- to introduce the main character, and perhaps one or two others
- to engage the reader's sympathy for one of the characters, make them care what happens
- to establish the time and place
- to make the reader feel that something good is coming.

Preparing for what follows

If you start with a dramatic event, make sure you can follow it with something better. If it's the most dramatic event in the story the rest is a let-down. Novels need variations, ups and downs in the level of intensity, but the main crisis should be as near the end as possible.

Don't confuse the readers

If you are introduced to a dozen strangers at once, can you remember all their names? Don't bring in too many characters to begin with, or the reader will be confused. They need time to absorb what to them is new information.

It isn't necessary to explain everything at the start. If you pose sufficiently intriguing questions the reader will want to continue in order to find the answers.

Coming back to it

If your beginning isn't right, don't get bogged down. A frequent reason for not completing a novel is that the would-be writer spends all his time perfecting the beginning, and never gets past chapter one.

Carry on, write the rest of the book, and come back to the beginning later. Many authors do it last of all, since a later incident can often suggest the ideal opening.

Action point

Practise writing good openings. It doesn't have to be a real novel you are working on, but develop ideas as they come, and file them for future possible use.

CASE STUDIES: OVERCOMING FIRST HURDLES

Sally has the wrong viewpoint

'I think you have Trisha eavesdropping too often,' Sally's friend says. 'Is it always necessary?'

'I've been worried about it myself,' Sally confesses. 'But she has to tell the reader certain things, and how else can she find out about them?'

'Letters? Perhaps not, people telephone so much these days there are fewer personal letters around.'

'Do you think it makes her look sneaky?'

'There is that. It's not how you want her to look. And as she's telling the story readers know she wasn't killed. They can't be frightened for her.'

'Do I have to give up the idea?'

'You'll get over most of the problems if you make it third person – you know, he and she instead of I – and then you can also let the reader know things Trisha doesn't.'

Sally hasn't chosen the most appropriate viewpoint.

Don tries to be too perfect

'How much more have you done?' Don's wife asks. He has spent several hours in the spare room where he has set up his desk.

Don sighs. 'I still can't get the first chapter right. Every time I look at it I can see things that need changing. I must have rewritten it ten times, and I'm still not satisfied. I'll never finish at this rate.'

'Don't you think it will help if you do a few more chapters? That might get you deeper into the story, and you'll be more confident about the first chapter, perhaps.'

Don tries this, and several weeks later he goes back to the first chapter and sees immediately that he has actually started too soon. Most of it is explained later, and he's able to cut almost all of the first twenty pages.

By carrying on he's beginning to treat the story as a whole and not get too bogged down.

Bridget's characters are too passive

'That's a lovely description of Eleanor and her house,' Bridget's sister says. 'But somehow, I'm not quite sure why, it isn't very lively. It reads a bit like an estate agent's brochure, or a description of a stately home in one of the county magazines, describing one room after another.'

'Could I have Eleanor showing someone round?'

'That would be better, she could be describing it. But who? And why are they being shown round?'

Bridget sighs. 'I don't know, everyone else in the story already knows the house. I can't bring in a new character just for that.'

'You could split it up, describe bits of the house at different times when some action takes place there. You can use things, they can play with that wonderful chess set, and sleep in the four-poster bed, and go and look at the portraits to see which person Eleanor resembles.'

Bridget manages to make her characters actively involved with their surroundings, so that the descriptions don't slow down the pace too much.

DISCUSSION POINTS

1. Take a dozen titles and see if you can discover where the authors found them. Are they appropriate, and what do they say about the contents, type or style of the books?

2. Look really closely at several novels. Can you find anything distinctive about the writing, the treatment of characters, ways of expressing things, humour, or imagery which gives the writers a special or unusual 'voice'?

3. Look at the checklist on the functions of the first page. Apply these to several novels, some you have read and some new to you, chosen at random. How far have the writers succeeded in doing everything? If they haven't in some cases, can you suggest reasons?

5
Looks and Language

PRESENTATION MATTERS

Your manuscript will not yet be ready for submission, but start to set your work out in the conventional manner so that it becomes normal to you. It will save time later.

First impressions

We are tempted to judge people on first impressions. They may be wrong, but it is difficult to overcome them. To give your manuscript the maximum chance of success, an agent's or an editor's first impression of it must be favourable. Their offices are very busy, they have many submissions, and may be able to spare very little time for each. Anything which looks scruffy or difficult or unprofessional could well be sent straight back unread.

Every agent and editor said that the presentation of a manuscript was important.

- 'It needs to be clean, double spacing, one side of the page and *not* heavily edited in pen by the side.' (Judy Piatkus)

- 'A well produced typescript suggests that the author cares about his/ her work and is at least trying to be professional.' (Michael Legat)

- 'If it appears that an author does not care about their manuscript, then why should an editor? I have been severely put off novels that are littered with spelling mistakes or scribbles.' (Luigi Bonomi)

Make it as clean, neat and professional as possible. It is counter-productive to devise elaborate covering sheets, provide pictures of possible covers, or huge-lettered title pages in an attempt to make it look like a real book. This shrieks of the amateur who is afraid his manuscript will not be good enough on its own and needs props.

The props hinder rather than help.

The right layout

Some publishers may ask for a copy on computer disk ready for publication, but don't send one first.

- (I dislike scripts) 'submitted on disk without a hard copy.' (Barbara Boote)

A manuscript must be typed, or word processed, using an average size (**pica** or ten letters to the inch) type, in a clear **font**, one which isn't so fancy it's difficult to read. Use the same font and size throughout. Use a black ribbon, and when it fades renew it. If your printer is dot-matrix don't use the draft mode which tends to be very faint.

The lines should be double spaced, and with wide (2–3cm) margins all round. This allows future editorial changes to be written in, or instructions to the typesetter.

With these margins you will normally have twenty-eight to thirty lines per page, between ten and twelve words per line. Use A4-sized white paper, preferably 80 gram weight so that the page beneath doesn't show through.

Pages should be numbered consecutively throughout, not starting each new chapter with page one.

Checklist

You need a title page with:

- your name and address and a daytime telephone number
- pseudonym if you are using one
- the book's title
- the approximate number of words.

Also:

- put your address on the final page too
- you can put your name and title at the top or bottom of each page, but make it clear this is not part of the text by having a line or a space between it and the text.

Pseudonyms

People use **pseudonyms** for many reasons. Their own name might be *[handwritten annotations, upper left:]* Marina Oliver

Text: set 12/14 pt Rommier 'unjustified'
X 24 pica measure X 36 lines
18pt Rommier initial for first letter on
chap. drop forward by text rule, others –
s. cap for first word
set text in 12 &
align with
18 pt cap   18 pt Perpera bold
                   u/lc. centre n
                   from TL4

THE GLOWING HOURS

BY

MARINA OLIVER

[handwritten:] fresh recto
start
arabic
numbering

[handwritten:] chapter title (A) CHAPTER ONE (TL4)

[handwritten:] NOTE TO PRINTER
–12e spacing?
throughout

[handwritten margin: f.c / T13]

'Ain't none on yer comin'?'

Nell, poised astride the narrow windowsill, stuffed her
ragged petticoat into the red flannel bloomers. She looked over
her shoulder. Nine pairs of eyes, some envious, most
apprehensive, stared back at her. How defeated they looked, she
thought with a spurt of irritation. They were so passive, so
unwilling to fight. Little red-haired Amy was the only one ever
to show a scrap of spirit, and she'd soon have it beaten out of
her. Then she was ashamed of her scorn. They hadn't had any
chance to experience a different sort of life. How could they
know it was possible to live without endless anger and violence?
She was the eldest of the girls, and had only recently summoned
up the courage to rebel.

No one spoke, and with a shrug she grasped the rope made
from a rough, almost threadbare blanket, tied to the brass
bedstead, and swung her leg out. 'Yer'll rue it,' she warned, *[handwritten: then hissed]*
'Shut winder, mind, Danny,' she hissed as she slid part way down
the rope. The frighteningly familiar thumps and bangs from the
room beneath ceased, and heavy footsteps could be heard

[handwritten margin left:] single
quotes
throughout
double
within
single

1

too difficult, not sound right, they prefer anonymity, or write more than one type of book.

Counting words

With computers it is possible to count the precise numbers of words, but this is misleading. A book with lots of short dialogue and many chapters will occupy more space than one with little dialogue and a few long chapters. It's the total pages the book will have that interests a publisher, so that he can work out printing and typesetting costs.

To calculate total **wordage** take the average number of words in ten complete lines, say 12, multiply by the number of lines in a complete page, say 30, then by the total number of manuscript pages, 300. 12 x 30 x 300 = 108,000 words. 'Approx 110,000 words' on your title page is enough.

Action point

Check several of your own pages, properly laid out as in Figure 5, and find out your average number of words per page.

Page layout

Indent all paragraphs, apart from the first ones in the chapter and after a break, which in a printed book will be indicated by a space. You can show a break by some mark such as * * *. The indentation should be big enough to make it perfectly clear it is a new paragraph; five spaces or the first pre-set tab is usual.

Don't, as in non-indented business correspondence, leave extra spaces between paragraphs.

In dialogue each new speaker must have a new paragraph, indented. You can put the spoken words after some introduction, without starting a new paragraph, if the introduction leads up to the speech. For example:

John looked at her and sighed. 'Come here,' he said.

Publishers have house styles for details such as single or double inverted commas, so unless you know which publisher you are writing for you can't know which to use. Just be consistent.

Helping the editor

You want to make it easy for editors to handle your work, as well as making it look professional.

Marina Oliver

The Laurels

High Town

Midshire

Tel: 019 876 5432

A CLANDESTINE AFFAIR

by

SALLY JAMES
(Pseudonym of MARINA OLIVER)

Approx 60,000 words

Fig. 3. A title page.

Checklist: Sending a manuscript

● Never pin or fasten pages together. Stabbed, bleeding editors are not receptive ones.

● Don't put pages in a ring binder. Editors tend to read on trains or at home, where a heavy manuscript which can't be split up into convenient sections is a nuisance.

● A rubber band or envelope folder is enough to keep pages together and tidy.

● Send the manuscript in a strong padded envelope. Ordinary envelopes tend to split if the parcel is heavy.

● Don't use lots of string, fancy knots, or lashings of sticky tape. By the time editors have fought their way in they aren't in the mood for kind judgements.

● Include a simple covering letter and return postage. Editors and agents are sensitive too. They could throw away submissions without return postage, or 'otherwise the agent or publisher has to ask for it, which is embarrassing.' (Laura Longrigg)

● A big, self-stick, self-addressed return label is easier than including another padded envelope.

● Always keep a copy of what you have sent. It doesn't happen often, but manuscripts can be lost.

MAKING LANGUAGE WORK FOR YOU

The way a writer uses vocabulary, sentence structure and imagery is part of her style. Aim for clarity, conciseness, precision and simplicity. Vary sentence and paragraph length and avoid a monotonous rhythm or construction.

Beginners allow language to become extravagant in the mistaken belief that this is 'literary'. They use too many adjectives and adverbs, produce over-elaborate descriptions, and concentrate on finding esoteric words instead of the most appropriate. They litter their work with strained imagery and obscure allusions. This is overwriting.

THE WRONG LAYOUT

'You can't expect me to swing that heavy handle,' Kitty said disbelievingly.

'Darling, be sensible! It's the only way to start the motor,' Timothy replied.

'But it's heavy!' 'Not as bad as you imagine. Come on, try it.'

'I have my new dress on.'

'And when you go driving you'll always have good clothes on. You can keep it out of the way.'

Reluctantly Kitty climbed down from the driving seat and took the starting handle in a fastidious grasp.

Fig. 4. An example of poor layout.

THE RIGHT LAYOUT

'You can't expect me to swing that heavy handle,' Kitty said disbelievingly.

'Darling, be sensible! It's the only way to start the motor,' Timothy replied.

'But it's heavy!'

'Not as bad as you imagine. Come on, try it.'

'I have my new dress on.'

'And when you go driving you'll always have good clothes on. You can keep it out of the way.'

Reluctantly Kitty climbed down from the driving seat and took the starting handle in a fastidious grasp.

Fig. 5. An example of good layout.
From *The Glowing Hours* by Marina Oliver.

Using language effectively

These writers have forgotten they are in the business of communication. If we want our work to be read with appreciation and understood correctly we need to use language as effectively as possible.

Agents reject:

- 'poor writing' (Sarah Molloy)
- 'bad English . . . overwritten situations, too many adjectives.' (Bob Tanner)

Editors appreciate:

- 'tight writing' (Beverley Cousins)
- 'a powerful writing style.' (Luigi Bonomi)

USING GRAMMAR, PUNCTUATION AND SPELLING

Tools to make our work easier

Some schoolteachers and creative writing tutors maintain that what is said is more important than the manner of its saying. They extol imagination, creativity and self-expression, and condemn any attempts to impose what they despise as 'restrictive rules and conventions' on this undisciplined outpouring.

They've missed the point.

Grammar and punctuation and spelling are not pedantic requirements which can safely be ignored. They are tools which help us to convey our thoughts accurately and unambiguously. We are speaking the same language as our listeners, and helping them to understand what we say with greater ease and fewer distractions. Anything which causes the reader to pause, try to work out what was meant, or go back and see whether that really was what the writer intended to say, is poor communication.

- 'I . . . always like an author who uses words well and understands grammar and punctuation and can spell.' (Michael Legat)

- A pet hate is 'bad spelling.' (Barbara Boote).

A practical consideration

Editors faced with two novels of equal interest, but room in their list for one, will choose the one which gives them less work correcting grammatical and other mistakes.

Action points: books to get
1. You probably already have a dictionary. A spelling dictionary, or a specialised writer's dictionary, as well as a dictionary of synonyms would also be useful.

2. If you are in the least unsure of grammatical rules and punctuation conventions, get a simple grammar book. Several are recommended in the reading list at the end of this book.

A reviewer commented: 'Often a less accomplished writer has grammatical tics which show up promiscuously – in the dialogue of many different characters as well as in the narrative.' Watch out for your own.

USING VOCABULARY, SLANG AND DIALECT

Choosing the most effective words
Aim for brevity and lucidity. A strong verb is better than a qualifying adverb. 'He strolled' is more vivid than 'he walked slowly'. An exact noun is better than a dozen adjectives. 'Iceberg' is better than 'a large, floating lump of frozen seawater'.

Of course this does not mean you can never use adverbs and adjectives, but use them sparingly, and when you are revising make sure each one is necessary. Watch for the phrases that are so common they have become clichés – like 'bouncing baby' or 'brakes squealing'.

Being wary of modifiers
When an adverb or adjective comes before the verb or noun it is **modifying**, particularly if there are several intervening words; it is weak, since we don't yet know what it is modifying. Words like rather, quite, a little, also weaken the effect. 'She was rather beautiful', and 'he was quite angry' are not very forceful or interesting comments.

Being positive
Show characters experiencing the external world and use specific examples instead of generalisations. Instead of 'it was very windy', you can convey the information more vividly if you have the wind blow a leaf into a character's face. Avoid passive verbs and tenses. 'He watched' is more forceful than 'he was watching'. 'He frowned' is better than 'he looked annoyed'. 'The dog barked' is more direct than 'there was a sound of a dog barking'.

Slang gets dated

Unless you want to illustrate that your novel takes place in a particular time or section of society, avoid slang. Even a couple of years later it can sound very odd, and what was current when you wrote your novel could be out of date by the time the book is in the shops.

- (I don't like) 'too much slang.' (Bob Tanner)

It has become fashionable with some kinds of books to use profanities and obscenities very freely. Authors may feel they are being realistic or liberated, but even these words have to be used by the appropriate characters – not everyone uses them or likes them.

- (I don't like) 'swear words.' (Barbara Boote)

Pronunciation and dialect

It's always difficult to decide whether to portray regional, or foreign or uneducated speech with phonetic spelling, and apostrophes indicating missing letters. Reading pages and pages of such speech can be very irritating, and it's better to hint at it than try to reproduce it accurately.

A similar problem occurs with dialect and foreign words. Too many hide the meaning from readers unfamiliar with them. A few words, intelligible from the context, are enough to give the flavour of the region or person.

- One reviewer disliked 'epigrams in foreign, untranslated, languages.'

With historicals you need to avoid modern terms, but also too many archaic ones like prithee and forsooth.

In all three situations turns of phrase, changing the order of words in a sentence, or different patterns and rhythms of speech can do the job more effectively.

USING DIALOGUE

Novels need dialogue. You have to solve an apparent contradiction. It is not ordinary speech with hesitations, repetitions, pauses, interruptions in trains of thought and confused explanations, but it must sound natural. Omit irrelevant chit-chat, and lengthy discussions or arrangements concerning actions which will be shown later.

- 'Ordinary speech copied straight onto the page will sound, as anyone who has read a transcript of a live broadcast will confirm, ungrammatical and barely literate.' (Reay Tannahill)

Remember that your characters will talk differently to different people. Their way of talking to a child, for instance, will not be the same as how they talk to adults, and they might abuse or tease close friends or relatives in a way they wouldn't their boss or a stranger.

Checklist
Dialogue has many functions. It should:

- provide information
- reveal the characters of both speaker and hearer
- move the plot forward
- show the mood of the speaker
- reveal likes and dislikes, attitudes and beliefs
- reveal what has happened, and what might happen
- create suspense, bring about crises, or solve difficulties.

- 'Every line of dialogue should work at least twice.' (Joan Hessayon)

Managing dialogue
You can read it aloud or into a tape recorder to judge whether it sounds real, neither stilted nor too formal.

- 'Speak it aloud in front of a mirror (like Dickens).' (Andrew Puckett)

Remember we choose different words and tend to use shorter sentences when we talk, compared with writing.

Your characters will have special habits, ways of speaking, which will help to make them distinctive.

Normally speeches will be short, one thought at a time.

Speakers are identified by tags: 'he said', 'Mary said', 'the doctor said'. The word said is almost invisible, but contrived synonyms such as uttered or related become intrusive. Use alternative words only when they are informative, such as muttered or shouted, though even here the manner of speaking should be obvious from the general atmosphere or the actual words said.

Sometimes it is clear from the order or the context who is

speaking, but the occasional reminder keeps the reader on track, and is essential with more than two speakers.

Action point
Write out a conversation with three speakers, making each speaker identifiable without speech tags, by their styles of speech or their opinions.

CASE STUDIES: DIFFICULTIES WITH LANGUAGE

Sally overwrites
Sally is correcting her first assignment from a writing class she has joined.

'It isn't very descriptive,' she thinks, and every time she comes to a noun she adds two or three adjectives. Then she adds adverbs to every verb. 'That's better, it makes it longer too,' she says to a friend from the class. 'I didn't think I'd be able to do the amount the tutor suggested.'

Sally is disappointed when her tutor shakes his head.

'This isn't the right way to be descriptive,' he tells her. 'Instead of "The trees had many thick green leaves" say "The lush foliage". It means the same, is shorter, and less boring. And instead of "She walked towards her appointment slowly, hesitantly and reluctantly, trying to find good, plausible and reasonable excuses for turning back" say "She lingered on the way." You've already told us she doesn't want to go and meet the fellow.'

Sally needs to be more precise.

Don listens
Don is still driving his taxi and he begins to listen to the customers, when they talk to him and when two passengers talk together. He discovers that he has a good memory for accents and the ways people speak.

He begins to put scraps of conversations he has overheard into his writing, and soon he finds that he can hear inside his head the way he wants his characters to speak. He knows how they pronounce words and which words they will use. He also realises that some people put the words in a different order, or emphasise certain words or syllables.

His dialogue becomes much more alive and interesting.

Bridget tackles her spelling

'I was always bad at spelling certain words, and tended to avoid them or use others,' Bridget says to her sister. 'I can't get away with that now. I muddle up double letters and never know whether endings are -ance or -ence. When I try to learn them I just get more confused. I'm too old for learning spellings.'

'Doesn't your computer have a spell-checker?'

'Yes, but it has American spelling, and it doesn't like proper names or abbreviations, and effect and affect are both good words so it doesn't know which I mean!'

'You know which words you are likely to get wrong. Do you always look them up?'

'I try to, but my dictionary is so heavy.'

'Then find a new trick. I'll buy you a small spelling dictionary and you make lists of the words you get wrong all the time and pin them up somewhere handy.'

Bridget is finding ways of overcoming problems.

DISCUSSION POINTS

1. Some bad writing gets published, but that doesn't eliminate the need to make yours as good as possible. Find examples you don't like of overwriting, too much dialect and outdated slang, and try to think of ways of improving them.

2. Analyse short conversations in books and note what every speech does, whether it serves two or more functions.

3. How much formal grammar can you remember from school? Are you aware of any personal quirks or faults? If so make a list. Have you ever consulted a grammar book, or one on style? Do you think doing so might be of help?

6
Setting the Scene

PAYING ATTENTION TO DETAIL

This relates to research, and also to the accuracy and notekeeping which is necessary.

Checklist: places

• Try to visit any real places you use for background.

• Get large-scale maps, check one-way streets and pedestrian precincts, the location of public buildings and hotels. If your story is set in the past get a map as close as possible to the year of the story.

• If your characters look out of a window at a distant range of hills, make sure it's possible to see them.

• Check they can catch trains to wherever they're going.

• Check the time it takes to travel by car or train or bus. If you guess wrongly, someone will know.

If you make a mistake you immediately lose your reader, who will not trust anything else you tell her.

Checklist: clothes

• Use clothes, cars and accessories which add to what we know about the characters. They must be realistic.

• If your heroine wears a designer dress is it because:
  a) she's rich and fashionable
  b) she bought it in a charity or nearly-new shop, or
  c) someone, maybe an employer, gave it to her?

- If someone always wears red, or black, or pale pink or scruffy jeans, why? What does it tell us about them? Describing your characters' clothes helps readers to visualise them and know them better, but be careful. Too much detail may be irrelevant and hold up the story.

CHECKING THE FACTS

As well as making sure all the factual detail is accurate, keep notes on details you have invented. This can include background facts which belong to the character profiles, but which you may not have thought of to begin with, such as additional family members, a childhood illness or accident, what they do as the story progresses, what information they have about others, or their beliefs and attitudes. In films continuity staff do this. Make notes as you go, or when re-reading your work.

Checklist: Continuity
- Record such permanent details as colours of eyes and hair, and other physical features in your character profiles, so that you can remind yourself when necessary.

- When information is revealed make a note, and also put down which characters already know the facts, or when they learn them, so that you don't have someone acting on the basis of something they couldn't have known.

- Keep track of the time of day, the days of the week, the passing seasons. Make sure the right flowers are blooming, and children are in school in October.

- In some books it feels as though there are a hundred hours in a single day. If you have characters doing a lot make sure it's physically possible for them to fit it into the time. This sounds obvious, but in the excitement of the writing it's easy to overlook.

- Don't let a pregnancy continue for two years.

- If there is a long time-scale keep track of the ages and make sure all the characters age by the same amount.

TEASING THE SENSES

As with other details, use references to what we experience through our senses, to enhance our knowledge of the characters or create a special mood or atmosphere.

The senses most involved will be seeing and hearing, but don't limit yourself to the obvious. Sudden sights of particular things bring back memories, as can hearing a tune or smelling something associated with a previous experience. Use this device to introduce a fact or recollection.

Make the characters active, experiencing things. Show someone stroking velvet, or a cat or a rose petal, or choking on dust, or shivering in the snow, rather than just describing the presence of velvet, or dust or snow.

Action point

Whenever you describe something try to see if it could be done more effectively through something a character does.

USING DESCRIPTION AND FLASHBACKS

These are essential devices but they pall with too much use.

Making description unobtrusive

Narrative combines dialogue and description, and the pace is usually faster during dialogue. Readers may skip long pages of unbroken description, but if it is slipped in as part of the action it is absorbed almost without being noticed.

If you want to describe scenery or buildings do it through the eyes of a character who sees it for the first time, or with some powerful emotion such as relief at returning home. The character who notices that a tree has been cut down and opened up some vista, or wanders round a room touching new and familiar objects, can convey so much more, and succinctly, about himself as well as the surroundings, than an outsider's account which can read like an inventory. Much the same applies to seeing people.

Accounts of events are much more dramatic if your characters are directly involved, experiencing them. Your story will be most effective if you mix the straightforward description with dialogue and the reactions of characters.

Hints and suggestions

Often these are more effective than a simple account. The reader can use her own imagination to fill the gaps, and is more involved in the story. She may also have a more vivid imagination than can be provided by any verbal description. This applies especially to scenes of violence and sex. It can be more horrific to focus on surrounding details of normality than to describe the physical specifics of an execution. It can be more erotic to suggest sexual tension and fulfilment than to go into minute clinical detail, which inevitably becomes repetitive.

* 'It's not necessary to include graphic details of violence if you don't feel happy writing them. It's sometimes more effective to suggest, or give just one grisly detail.' (Ann Hulme)

* 'Everyone agreed that they dislike the "purple passages" often found in today's novels. Bring back the asterisk!' (Louth Writers' Circle)

Showing, not telling

This is advice frequently given to aspiring writers. Quite simply **showing** means getting inside your characters, and presenting the action and emotion as they experience it. This involves devising scenes. **Telling** is narrating from outside, as if you are the audience looking down on a stage, experiencing everything at second, not first hand. There are times, however, when a little discreet telling is necessary, briefer and better than an awkward, contrived scene which lasts for half-a-dozen swift exchanges.

Exposition

This is a type of description when an explanation is necessary. The writer breaks away from the scene to give the background, some essential information, or a summary of events leading up to it.

It slows the action, and is distancing. Readers will be interested only if they feel it is relevant, and want to know. As with other description it can be more effective if built into the action, but sometimes it would be false if characters amicably discuss something they know perfectly well, like who inherited Aunt Dottie's money. If they are the right sort of people, and it fits your story, you could convey this information by having them row about it. Or they could explain it to a stranger, but only if he has some interest. If these devices are not possible it may have to be simple telling.

Flashbacks

These are scenes from the past, and are often used from a desire to show and not tell. They tend to be overused. They stop the action, can be confusing, and prevent the reader from getting on with the story to come, which is usually more interesting to her.

- 'Not too many flashbacks which interrupt continuity.' (Ruislip Literary Society)

When they are used make certain the reader knows it's a flashback, and when it starts and finishes. A frequent method is to have a character remember something, prompted by what happens now, drop into the flashback scene as if experiencing it, then return to the original scene.

The switch can be within the character's thoughts, as he recalls it, but shown in 'real time' as though it's happening now. Or the character could say something like 'That reminds me of the time when . . .', and then the flashback drops into real time instead of having the characters talking about it having happened in the past.

It will finish either at the end of a scene or chapter, or if it's a short one contained within another scene, by making it perfectly clear we are back in the main story. There are various ways of doing this: by referring to the flashback as something in the past, or switching back to a character present in the main scene but not in the flashback, or by picking up the action or conversation which was interrupted by the flashback.

Flashbacks must be interesting in themselves. The reader wants to get on with what's happening *now*, and will lose interest and patience if she is bored by a lengthy flashback which she doesn't perceive as relevant to now.

Action point

Analyse flashbacks in a book, see how each is introduced, how long it is, how it is concluded. Was it necessary or could it have been done differently?

Flashes forward

These are often prologues which are extracts from later in the book, but also can come as hints of future events. They need to be done very carefully as pointers. Have, for example, a character planning what to do or looking forward to better times. Avoid at all costs the heavy-handed authorial interjection of such predictions as 'she didn't know that next year she would have lost everything.'

• A pet hate: 'Little did I know that...' (Michael Legat)

THE MIDDLE MUST BE COMPULSIVE READING

It can be comparatively simple to write beginnings and ends. Middles distinguish good writers from average ones. You must keep up the momentum of the story, make the reader stay with you, eager to know the outcome. It's fatally easy to lose one's way, having too little to say or padding with more and more incidents which don't help the story.

When I asked what made a good novel, most people said a convincing plot and good characters, but also:

• 'One which instructs, reveals, stimulates thought, but above all, entertains. One which leaves a glow. One which you are prepared to recommend to others.' (Andrew Puckett)

• 'A well-constructed, well-written story, which is enjoyable as a story, but which is also intellectually stimulating.' (Hilary Johnson)

• 'Intelligently written and plotted.' (Sarah Molloy)

• 'Gripping storyline.' (Lynn Sanders)

• 'Gripping first chapter.' (Tracy Long)

• 'The plot. This gets me interested but the writing and characters have to be believable or my interest will not be held.' (Mary Wilson)

• 'Setting – either local or exotic settings always popular. Action needs to be plausible as well as exciting – suspension of disbelief.' (Christine Budworth)

• 'Story should keep going at a good pace, not get bogged down by too much description.' (Anne Ambler)

• 'Strong storyline with a fast pace to keep the reader interested.' (Sue Richardson)

- 'Keeps the reader turning the pages.' (Deborah Smith)

- 'One that keeps me reading even when there are many more pressing things to do.' (Haydn Middleton)

- 'One which you cannot put down' (Susan Sallis)

- 'One I want to continue reading.' (Jane Morpeth)

- 'Writing that blisters your spirit with delight (a plot that keeps you on tenterhooks until the end).' (Sara Banerji)

- 'One that makes me escape into the world of that novel and makes me believe in the novel itself. I want to continue with that novel.' (Luigi Bonomi)

- 'One that keeps me turning each page to the end. (Dorothy Lumley)

- 'I like to think it educates me in a subject that interests me.' (Judy Phillips)

- 'One which, after you have finished reading stays in the mind and memory.' (Frederick Nolan)

- 'It has to keep you glued to it either with suspense or in tears.' (Diane Allen)

- 'Something that makes me miss my tube stop.' (Barbara Boote)

- 'A good novel is one that works *for the reader* on every level – and that is nearly always the result of dedicated and detailed technical proficiency; precise control of words, structure and pace, characterisation based on knowledge of what makes people tick, a quality of imaginative vitality that transcends clichés of speech and thought...All these are definable. What isn't definable is the rare and special authorial spark that makes the difference between a competent novel and a brilliant one.' (Reay Tannahill)

Whether you plan the whole story in detail or let your characters and plot develop, you need to be aware of the overall shape. I look at this in the next chapter.

USEFUL REFERENCE BOOKS

As you write more you will build a library of the books used most frequently. Some are general, but you will have special interests depending on the type of novel you write, such as historical or crime. If you use a multi-media computer CDs are available, and soon we'll all be using the Internet, but books may still be preferred by many people.

Checklist: Books to look for

- A good encyclopaedia and a dictionary, as big as you can afford, are investments. You will be consulting them far more frequently than you imagine.

- One of the yearbooks for writers, the *Writers' and Artists' Yearbook* or *The Writer's Handbook*, even an out of date one, will be of value as both give lengthy lists of agents and publishers.

- Spelling dictionaries are quicker to use than an ordinary one.

- A thesaurus or book of synonyms will help you to avoid repeating words.

- A dictionary of names will give you ideas, and telephone directories are useful in saving you from calling all your minor characters John and Mary Jones.

- A book of quotations can provide ideas and titles.

- Books on grammar, punctuation and style.

- Books by writers about their own experiences and discoveries are useful and often fascinating.

- There are many specialist guides and 'how to' books to help with particular types of writing.

- Maps, guidebooks, and pamphlets, as well as hotel directories, will provide many local details.

- There are numerous small books on a huge variety of subjects, like the Shire books, detailed enough to tell you the basics without being too technical and overwhelming.

● Don't ignore books for children, either. They can be excellent in giving the real core of a subject.

Action point
Look in a large bookshop and make a list of the reference books you would like to acquire. Could these go on a birthday present list?

CASE STUDIES: DEALING WITH THE FACTS

Sally gets confused
Sally asks a friend to read the chapters she has done so far.

'I like your arrogant hero,' Caroline says, 'but has he got dark or blond hair? It was dark at the beginning, and here on page twenty it's fair. And you say he's been to Eton, but he mentions girls in the same class. Do they have girls there? And would he be so macho if he's been to a mixed school? Oh, and you say your heroine was an only child but on page thirty you mention her sister.'

Sally groans. 'I didn't check. I'll have to change a lot. I wish I'd thought about this earlier.'

Sally is enjoying writing her novel so much that she doesn't stop to make notes or do research. It gives her a lot of extra work in the end.

Don gets carried away
Don has found a good plot and some believable characters, and is enjoying doing the dialogue. He thinks he's come to grips with what writing is about.

His characters go on a long journey, a route which Don knows well and always enjoys. He drives along the route and back, making lots of notes of details, and then writes a six-page description of what his characters will see.

His wife says it's boring. 'People will skip this,' she warns. 'You hardly mention the characters, they'll be forgotten, and readers don't like large chunks of description and no conversation, no action.'

'But it's beautiful scenery,' Don says, hurt.

'Well, you can still show some, but I think something else should happen.'

Don nods, and begins to think how he can combine the action with the description.

Bridget goes on location

'I want to see the town for myself,' she says to her sister.

'But you spent a weekend there a few years ago.'

'It might have changed, and I can't remember it all that well, despite the book I got out of the library.'

Bridget goes, and is so thankful when she realises that a new pedestrian precinct has been built, and she can't have her characters driving along that street. Also one of the hotels she has used from the guide book was destroyed by a fire two months ago. She missed the news report.

'So it was well worth it,' she tells her sister when she arrives back home. 'If I hadn't gone I'd have made some dreadful mistakes.'

DISCUSSION POINTS

1. Have you ever spotted a factual or continuity mistake in a book, or wondered whether something could be the way it was described? If so, how would you avoid the mistake?

2. Consider ways in which you can 'show, not tell' your scenes. Will it always work, and if you have to 'tell' can you do it briefly?

3. Do some books sag in the middle? Can you identify the reasons, and say how you would have avoided or got round the problems, to make the books tauter?

7
The Overall View

AVOIDING WRITER'S BLOCK

There are several versions of this phenomenon, being unable to write, and the solutions depend on the cause.

A traumatic event
An event like a bereavement can be a cause. Know that as time passes you will recover. For some people writing can in itself be healing or a therapy.

Inauspicious surroundings
This is difficult, but P. G. Wodehouse wrote half a novel with his typewriter perched on a suitcase, in the recreation room of a German internment camp surrounded by fifty men singing and playing games, with armed guards peering over his shoulder. He later wrote a chapter while in a police cell in Paris, and a hundred pages in hospital. You too can overcome disadvantages.

Just not feeling in the mood
This could be laziness, a disinclination to work, or have a deeper cause such as not wanting to work on the current project. Overcoming it is up to you and how determined you are to become a writer. Sit down and type (or write) anything. Reply to some letters which have been waiting around. If you have none just type nonsense, shopping lists, or copy some pages from a favourite book, or the last few pages you wrote. The act of typing often stimulates ideas and renewed enthusiasm.

Not knowing how to continue
This may be from lack of ideas, not knowing your characters well enough, too little plot, not enough or not a big enough conflict, or because you have dug yourself into a hole. Reading over what you've

done may produce ideas for the next scene. You may need to go back and make changes which will provide the answer. Relax, think about the problem just before you go to bed and let the subconscious work on it. You may have to abandon the project, at least for the moment. If you do, make sure you start something else right away. This will restore your confidence and keep you in practice.

Novelists give suggestions
- 'Keep going.' (Susan Sallis)

- 'Keep writing whatever and all problems will pass.' (Sara Banerji)

- 'Have a stiff gin.' (Anita Burgh)

- 'A novel's like a car engine. If it stops, then don't swear and bang your fists. Take it apart till you find the fault. If it's repairable, repair it. If it's beyond economical repair, burn it.' (Matthew Kneale)

- 'If a book blocks, start writing another of a different kind. When lying in bed before sleep, think clearly through a problem. It may solve itself while you sleep.' (Anne Melville)

- 'I don't believe in writer's block. There are times when it's harder than others: tough. Who said it was easy to start with? But there is a trick to getting a story moving if it's stuck, and that's to bring in an *important* new character.' (Philip Pullman)

Action point
Make a list of the reasons you've given yourself (or others) for not writing. Were they a hundred per cent truthful? *Creativity isn't the only activity.*

If the muse has deserted you, you can:

1. do research
2. read your notes
3. make more notes
4. tidy your notes or reorganise your filing system
5. go through your file of new ideas
6. make plans for future novels
7. catch up on a host of other 'office' tasks which you don't have

time for when being creative.

There is always some work to do, even if it's not writing. Many professionals say writer's block doesn't exist, and journalists with deadlines rarely suffer from it.

DIRECTING YOUR SCENES

Introduce main characters as soon as possible, preferably on the first page, because they are the ones readers want to know about. It's distracting and disappointing to have to switch attention to a different heroine when you assumed the first girl mentioned was the main protagonist.

Bring in all your important characters as soon as the plot allows, as early as you can in the context of the story. Be careful, though, not to introduce too many at once, or the reader becomes confused.

Never introduce any character with a potted biography. Most of their past lives will be irrelevant, and bore the reader. If some of their history is important you can bring in essential facts more subtly, as they are necessary for understanding the character or the situation. Just give a few relevant details which will help the reader remember them, and know why they are there, what their function is.

Don't drop hints or start trails and not follow them. If a one-eyed man looks over the garden wall and recognises the murderer, he must play some future part in the story. Your reader will be waiting for him to return.

Action point
Analyse a book and note when characters are introduced, and how much is said about them

1. then
2. later.

CONTROLLING THE PACE

Pace and rhythm vary from book to book, and within one book. Scenes, action and dialogue are more immediate than description. They create more tension. So does an intensive conflict. Jeopardy is something dire which is being anticipated, but it must be a possible outcome, within the conventions of the genre, to make the reader concerned.

Lots of short sentences and urgent action increase the pace. You can enhance a mood of peace or tension by externals like the weather, a storm or spectacular sunset.

Decide which are the big scenes and work towards them, build up anticipation, and spread them through the book. These scenes should be significant, and change the story or the character. They are likely to be long, so you could have a short, fast scene immediately before for contrast.

Don't stop in the middle of an exciting scene to explain something. You have to get the information in earlier so that the reader understands what's happening and the significance, or explain it later, if you can do so without it appearing like something you forgot to put in.

You can start in the middle of a scene, perhaps a quarrel, to increase the pace.

CONSIDERING THE OVERALL PATTERN

Plots and subplots

There will be one main thread concerning your chief characters, but there could be several subplots. The trick is to weave them all together so that the different strands converge and separate, meet and overlap, affect one another, mirror or contrast one another. Imagine each character as a different coloured ribbon. Some start at the top all tied together, then the ribbons are twisted or plaited together in an irregular way, others being inserted or cut off at different points. They form ever-changing patterns, taking greater or lesser prominence at different times, but the loose strands are tied, the problems solved or the resolutions found by the end of the book.

Let your readers become familiar with a minor character and interested in him, before you leave the main plot-line to follow his separate story.

Some subplots may be ended quite early, but make sure you don't introduce a subplot, concentrate exclusively on it, and solve it in a few pages. That destroys tension and anticipation. Instead prolong these by inserting bits of the subplot into the main narrative at intervals.

Don't introduce a subplot and forget to continue with it for so long that your readers have forgotten the details by the time you do. If the story demands that it is drawn out, be sure to mention it occasionally.

It helps to keep a list of your scenes, just a few brief words to remind you of what they did and who is taking part. Then you can see quickly if you've left one character or subplot out for too long, or concentrated too much on one subplot for a while at the expense of others.

Viewpoint patterns

When you have a complex plot you will often have a multi-viewpoint pattern, and you need to make smooth transitions from one viewpoint to another. When switching viewpoints make it clear at once, as with flashbacks, that there's a switch. It's very irritating to the reader if the 'he' of the second scene appears to be the same one from the first for several paragraphs.

There are many devices you can use

You can show a transition by a change of time. This can be a straight 'The next day' or a switch from dusk to midday sun.

A change of place can be shown similarly, with a change from a scene in a building to 'Back on the farm' or 'The boat swung broadside as they cast off'.

You can have a lead-in paragraph, such as a speech by a character who wasn't in the earlier scene.

You could have an echo from the first to the next scene, like a repeated word or phrase or action, perhaps by a different character, or you can use simple summary or exposition.

Being consistent

Indicate to the reader early on the pattern of viewpoint switching. If you change with each chapter or scene, do so at once, not halfway through the book, to get the reader accustomed to it.

Tell only what the viewpoint character can see, hear or experience. They can see another character laugh or frown or cry or shout, and assume from this his emotion, but they can't see inside his head and know precisely what he is thinking or what actions he is planning.

Shape

The **shape** of the novel will be a series of crises, each one built up to, then resolved. Some will be small, some huge. The resolution will often lead to a further complication and eventually another crisis, and all will lead to the major crisis or turning point, as close to the end as possible.

For example, there is a problem in the office, an order mislaid, so the boss stays on to sort it. He misses an appointment, or meets an old friend on the later train home. This could have vital consequences such as losing a contract, a row with his wife, the last straw which causes her to walk out, or getting involved in some

SUMMARY OF CHAPTERS – COBWEB CAGE
(by Marina Oliver)

DATE	Main Chars	
		CHAPTER ONE P 1
2/1901	M	Marigold alone, Poppy born, locked in pantry
2/01	MJyMyJ	Johnny finds her – discuss names
1/05	My	Ivy born – nightmares – flowers – names appropriate
12/08	J	pit accident
2/09	My	John home and ill – Mary goes to work
3/09	P	Poppy wants to go on choir outing
4/09	M I	Mrs Tasker brings Ivy home with pie – falls on fire.
		CHAPTER TWO P 35
4/09	Fam	Ivy's accident – burnt.
/10	M I	Ivy resists school – effects of burns on John – Johnny delicacies
3/11	Fam	Ivy draws – job for Marigold – Johnny meat, wants drawing Mary backache
5/11	Fam	Walk on hills – talk of unions and reforms
6/11	My	Mary home – pregnant – ill – Mrs Nugent calls – Mary miscarries
6/11	Jy	Johnny a thief – sent to job in Birmingham.
		CHAPTER THREE P 65
3/12	Fam,	Mine strike – army at Cannock
6/12	Fam	Poppy writes Johnny – Ivy drawing on it – Marigold job at Oxford
7/12	M	Marigold at Oxford
10/12	P	Ivy playing with Lizzie – brother says Poppy pretty
11/12	P	Poppy fantasising about house – wants to get away
12/12	M R	Marigold helps at dinner party – meets Richard.
		CHAPTER FOUR P 95
12/12	Fam	Boxing day – Johnny home – Mary worries losing him, & Poppy
12/12	M R	Walk with children – meet and talks to Richard
2/12	R S	Sophia at Baden Baden – Richard recalls why he's at Oxford now
12/12	I	Ivy playing doctors, breaks window
12/12	M R	Marigold and Richard walk by river
12/12	Jy	Johnny at work – tells Lucy about his thieving
12/12	M R	New Year, Richard drives Marigold home
		CHAPTER FIVE . P 129
12/12	Fam	Row over window, Ivy denies. Marigold sees poverty at home
12/12	R	Richard recalls his affair with Flo
1/13	Fam	John angry – has these attacks, then silent and morose
1/13	M R	Set off back to Oxford
1/13	My	Mary sees Marigold in motor car
2/13	M R	Talk on way back to Oxford – agree to meet again
2/13	R	Flo demands money because she is pregnant.

Fig. 6. Keeping track of scenes.

new development like industrial espionage or witnessing a crime. You can imagine the plot as a line on a graph, with the level of intensity on one axis, the progress of the novel along the other, and the plot moving in a series of peaks and troughs. If you have one or more subplots they will have similar peaks and troughs, but make sure you don't have all the peaks coming together – spread them out. (See Figures 7 and 8.)

KEEPING THE PAGES TURNING

As the earlier quotes show, authors, agents, editors and readers all say that wanting to get to the end, to see what happens to the characters is essential. They want to be drawn from page to page. It's the sign of a good storyteller when this happens, but storytelling is a difficult skill to learn. There are some pointers, apart from an intriguing plot and good characterisation.

Checklist
Readers will continue if:

- Your characters are interesting.
- What they are doing matters.
- Their aims are laudable.
- You are intriguing the reader, tempting her to want to know more about them and care what happens to them.
- Your plot is exciting, but plausible.
- Your plot has unexpected twists and turns.

Prolonging the suspense
You entice the reader further by continually posing fresh questions, to which she wants the answers, but in giving the answers you pose a further question. Don't explain everything at once. If a girl sees her lover in a compromising situation and he explains how innocent it all was in the next scene, and she believes him, there would be little tension. If the police catch the murderer leaving the scene of the crime covered in blood and carrying the blunt instrument, there is no mystery. If the starship obliterates the competitor in chapter one there is no race.

Suspense is created in this way, also by making promises to your reader, by how the story starts and what expectations you arouse, that the book will be exciting or thrilling. Readers become involved as the characters they like face dangers or suffering. They can be

Fig. 7. The peaks and troughs of one plot.

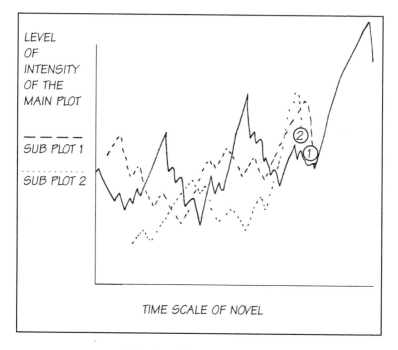

Fig. 8. Adding two subplots.

angry at some injustice. The pressure of a time-factor enhances suspense.

Readers keep turning the pages if:

- 'The author is able to generate a sense of excitement and discovery in me.' (Barbara Levy)

- 'To find the answer to "What happened next".' (Jill Black)

- 'There is 'the tingle factor' and 'narrative tension.' (Hilary Johnson)

- There is 'some "mystery"': will she get her man, will he escape the hidden menace, will they find the murderer?' (Laura Longrigg)

- 'Characters, storytelling, humour, writing style.' (Caroline Sheldon)

- 'Readability. Getting me involved with the characters, caring about them.' (Dorothy Lumley)

- 'Strong, well written characters with plausible plot.' (Diane Allen)

- 'Witty, fast writing, a sense of tension and being hooked into various characters.' (Luigi Bonomi)

- 'Strong characters, and a plot that twists and turns unexpectedly, but never unreasonably.' (Michael Legat)

CLIFFHANGING TECHNIQUES

A favourite way of ending a chapter is the **cliffhanger**, where your characters are left in a desperate situation and the reader, almost without noticing, passes on to the next chapter in order to see what happens. It creates suspense.

You can use the same technique at the ends of scenes. It won't always be explained immediately in the following chapter or scene, which may switch to someone else, but the readers want to go on to find the answer.

You can do it in the middle of a scene by having interrupted events or conversations, unexplained hints and references, surprises, alternative possibilities with the choices not made at once.

WRITING A SATISFYING ENDING

Agents, editors and readers want to be able to put a book down with a sigh of satisfaction.

- 'When I finish that novel I feel a sense of completeness and deep satisfaction.' (Luigi Bonomi).

In some literary novels the outcome is hinted at rather than explained, and can be downbeat. In most other novels endings tend to be upbeat, and it's more satisfying for the reader to know what happened. Did the hero get the girl, the detective unmask the crook, the explorer return safely, the soldiers win the battle? How were these resolutions finally concluded?

Make certain all the ends you want to tie up are satisfactorily explained, and you haven't overlooked some vital piece of evidence in your relief at finishing.

A satisfying ending is not necessarily a happy one, but it must be logical, follow from what has gone before. You can connect the ending to the beginning with some allusion or repetition, but most endings reach a climax, the protagonists achieve some ambition, get what the reader feels they deserve after all their trials and endeavours.

Before you give your protagonists their ending, clear up all the other strands, tuck them in, and get the other characters off-stage. Leave the stage clear for this final scene, and make it a scene, action rather than discussion. Include essential explanation within the scene.

CASE STUDIES: FACING PROBLEMS

Sally fluffs her ending

'I've finished!' Sally says to her writing group. 'I've brought the last chapter to read.'

She reads the first few pages, where the hero and heroine meet accidentally on a train journey, and talk about their misunderstandings, then the group comments.

'They don't make it happen, it's a chance meeting.'

'And they can hardly have a good clinch on a crowded train. They should meet somewhere private.'

'But what about her sister and her broken engagement? Do they get together too? You don't say.'

'I was going to,' Saily says crossly, 'but Betty interrupted.'

'I thought it was the end, they've made it up.'

'I've still got several pages where the sister meets her man, and the neighbour's little boy is found alive.'

Sally has the wrong order, her ending is a let-down.

Don is breathless

Don sends his manuscript to an agent he's met at a party. He is disappointed when it comes back, with a letter saying that it was too exciting.

'How can it be *too* exciting?' he demands. 'Books are supposed to be full of suspense.'

'What else does he say?' his wife asks, taking the letter. 'Yes, I see. "You don't distinguish sufficiently between the big scenes and the others, you need to vary the pace and the intensity. But if you can work on this I'd be happy to look at it again." That sounds encouraging.'

'I don't think I'll bother. He doesn't want it.'

'I heard on the radio today that most publishers and agents are so busy they can only send a standard rejection slip. They don't ask to see it again unless they think it's worth it. So the least you can do is take his advice.'

Don has promise, but needs to work at his skills.

Bridget gets stuck

'My plot's too complicated, I can't see what I'm trying to do,' Bridget sighs.

She gives up writing, feeling discouraged, but keeps going back to sort out her notes, and one day she picks up her manuscript and reads it through.

'I wonder if that would work?' she asks suddenly. 'Yes, I can change this, put things in a different order, and have Charlotte find the letter, not Maisie. That will solve some of the problems.'

Her enthusiasm renewed, Bridget begins working and soon completes her manuscript.

DISCUSSION POINTS

1. Take your plot, or one you know well, and draw a diagram similar to the ones in this chapter of the peaks and troughs of the

main plot and any subplots.

2. Look at how you can insert essential information. Does dialogue, narrative, or straight exposition work best, or does it depend on the novel?

3. Analyse the endings of ten books you have read recently, and say why they are (or are not) satisfying.

8
Submitting Your Work

FINAL POLISHING

You've reached the end of your novel. Well done. You thought you had almost finished? I'm sorry, but there is still a great deal to do.

Don't spend too much time as you go
It's a great temptation to keep going back over what you've done. You can always find things to change. Even when a script has been completed, writers tinker. They are perhaps reluctant to let it go out into a hard, hostile world.

Try not to go back too much while doing the first draft, unless you get to a complete dead end and have to alter something vital for the plot to work. It's better to finish your first draft, prove you can write a whole novel, then start revising. Some writers revise as they go, but many do a very fast first draft and spend far longer on the revising stage. The experienced writer knows that revision, whenever done, is the most important, often most difficult task. Most writers I spoke to did three or more drafts.

● 'Write huge and cut harshly.' (Sara Banerji)

Taking a break
Put the script away for as long as possible, then come back refreshed. You can have a blitz on garden or housework, or go out and see all the friends you've been neglecting.

Keep on writing though. It's fatally easy to get out of the habit. You can write something else, short stories or non-fiction. Distance yourself from your novel, try to forget it, so that when you come back you can judge it objectively. Then try to read it as if you are new to the story.

Now for the really hard work
Revision can be done at several levels, and it's very like the editing

and copy-editing before a book is published.

You can start with the details, which is what a copy-editor does, or the overall view, the editor's task.

Action points: Correcting details

It's perhaps easiest at first to concentrate on:

1. Simple corrections of typing errors.

2. The changing of words which have been repeated too close together, or too often.

3. The removal of superfluous adverbs and adjectives, often replacing these phrases with more appropriate or effective verbs and nouns.

4. Checking for clichés, trite expressions, or convoluted metaphors.

   As you are doing this you may want to:

5. Change the order of words or passages.

6. Rewrite sentences.

7. Shift scenes around.

Checklist

Make sure everything is essential and important.

• Now might be the best time for a swift read-through, making notes as you go.

• Have you started in the right place, or too soon in the story?

• Look at each scene for its purpose. Does it move the story forward, demonstrate facets of character, tell the reader something relevant and new? If not, why is it there?

• Does the action come in the wrong place? Is the dialogue natural, interesting, necessary, informative? If not you may have to cut it out.

• You can do the same for each sentence. Cut out everything that isn't essential.

• Does the pace vary enough?

- Are some scenes too slow or boring?

- Have you exploited every situation and emotion fully?

- Is there too much exposition?

- Is anything missing, such as explanations or clues?

- Have you always chosen the right viewpoint or would a scene be better done from a different one?

- Are there too many flashbacks?

- Have you made it clear when you change viewpoint and have flashbacks?

- Are your big scenes in the right places?

- Does the story flow, the events easily understood by the reader?

- Is the resolution satisfactory, arising inevitably out of the story?

- Is every character essential? Could two minor ones be merged?

- Are the characters real, convincing?

- Are they in conflict?

- Do they develop, grow?

- Is their behaviour in line with their motivations?

- Check all the details, make sure you have been consistent, that the time-scale is correct.

- Is the language appropriate? Is it vivid and arresting?

- Have you used the senses?

- Is there any humour?

- Have you used active verbs?

- Have you used specific rather than general examples?

When you are satisfied with every aspect and have a clean,

corrected copy using the accepted layout as described earlier, you are ready to submit your work.

USING AN AGENT

Many authors do very well without an agent, but it is much easier to have one. The problem is that it can be as difficult to find an agent as it is to get the script accepted by a publisher. Both agents and publishers are in business, and need to pay their way. They must become good judges of what will sell if they want to remain in business.

Agents are in regular touch with editors and know what they like, or are looking for. Editors, knowing that agents will only pass on what they think is publishable, take submissions from agents more seriously than unsolicited ones. Agents negotiate contracts, and can sort out any later problems. They charge a percentage of your earnings, but usually get more for you to cover this.

Finding an agent

The ideal way is by recommendation through an existing client, but you won't necessarily know published writers and their agents may not be prepared to take on more clients.

There are lists in the yearbooks, and they often indicate whether agents specialise in particular types of work, names of some clients, whether they are accepting new clients, and if they want a query letter first.

Agents attend conferences, and give talks and workshops. You can meet them this way, though you won't be popular if, as at least one aspiring writer did, you pursue them into the loo and thrust scripts under the cubicle door. If you can find a new one just setting up, you might be taken on before their list is full.

Action point

Go through one of the yearbooks and make a list of at least ten prospective agents you might try.

ENTERING COMPETITIONS

The yearbooks have lists of prizes, some open to unpublished writers. There are often special conditions, such as a minimum or maximum age, or a regional connection. While the number of entries for these competitions can be in the hundreds, winning one is valuable for publicity as well as any monetary reward. Sometimes runners-up as well as at winners are offered publishing contracts.

Action point
Make lists of competitions you would be eligible for.

CHOOSING THE RIGHT PUBLISHER

When writing a novel you can write what you like and think about publication later, or aim your work at a particular publishing house from the start. Which you choose depends on the type of novel.

If you aim to write category fiction, romance novels for Harlequin Mills and Boon, for instance, you have to abide by very strict guidelines as to length, limits on the number of main characters, concentration on relationships and so on. The publishers send out guidelines for potential authors, and a tape full of useful advice. There are many such publishers of category romances in the USA, and they all want different things, so you need to know their requirements first or your chances of success are minimal.

● 'Be professional: do your homework – submit work to a house which publishes material of the same nature as your own.' (Deborah Smith)

● (Do your) 'market research, then use your own voice.' (Elizabeth Johnson)

● 'Select the publisher on the basis of the kind of books they publish.' (Richard Todd)

● 'My first published novel was rejected by fourteen publishers before being accepted. Conclusion: Determination is just as important as talent. (It would have helped, of course, to have taken more care in the choice of a suitable publisher.)' (Anne Melville)

Many publishers have several imprints, each usually publishing a limited range or type of book.

Action point
Make a list of the most likely publishers for your novel.

As with agents, there are sometimes new publishers and new imprints which will not have a ready-made list of authors, and will be more willing to consider newcomers. To hear about these opportunities you need to mix with other writers, to read the specialist magazines, to network.

PREPARING PROPOSALS, OUTLINES AND SYNOPSES

Query letters

If an agent or publisher specifies a preliminary letter, send it. Post, don't fax it. Anything else may come back unread and you will have wasted your postage. Always send return postage and a self-addressed envelope or label.

The letter is your introduction, the first impression the agent or editor will have of you, so it is important to make it as good as possible.

* 'The cover letter is more important (than the title).' (Barbara Levy)

* (I am looking for) 'professionalism in submission letter and presentation.' (Barbara Boote)

* 'Be professional in your approach to selling.' (Judy Piatkus)

It should be business-like, no more than a page, single spaced, saying what you have written, a two or three sentence summary of it, any relevant facts about yourself such as previous publications or special knowledge, and asking whether you might send sample chapters for consideration. You might add a reason for choosing that firm, to show you've done your homework, on the lines of they represent or publish lots of crime novelists and your script is a crime novel. But never flannel. Gushing, or sycophantic praise, will annoy rather than impress.

* (I dislike authors) 'trying to queue-jump, trying to get my attention by being rude, controversial or fawning in submission letters.' (Jane Morpeth)

Proposals

These are more likely to be required for non-fiction than for novels. Occasionally established authors may be commissioned on a proposal and a few chapters only for a novel, and one day you may need to make one.

Editors and agents have varying policies on accepting manuscripts on the basis of proposals. Agents are, perhaps understandably, more willing to try.

- 'If I thought it was good enough.' (Carole Blake)

- (Yes) 'but they would usually have to complete it before a publisher would be interested.' (Sarah Molloy)

- 'Unlikely.' (Jane Morpeth)

- 'Rarely. If highly commended by an agent, if a celebrity author.' (Barbara Boote)

- 'Probably only if the writer had a track record in another area, say journalism or TV.' (Barbara Levy)

and:

- 'Never. A few good chapters do not make a book. Many writers start off well and fall away, or appear to lose interest midway through a novel.' (Bob Tanner)

Proposals include an **outline**, a **synopsis**, a list of **contents** and **chapter headings**, and details of where you see the book fitting into the existing market.

Outlines
This is a very brief description, one page, of the story. It is something you might do when planning the story, with the chapters indicated and the main scenes listed.

Action point
For an exercise, do a proposal and outline for the book you have finished.

Synopses
These are quite different, and it is essential you study the art of writing them.

- (I like) 'a very easy to understand synopsis written in a clear style.' (Luigi Bonomi)

A synopsis should accompany your script, especially if you send a **partial**, that is the first few chapters only. A summary should be in narrative form, usually the present tense, two to four A4 pages double-spaced. They can be important to get you past the first hurdle. The synopsis is a practical aid to selling your script. It must tell the whole story and the conclusion. It is not, as many inexperienced writers believe, the same as the cover blurb which is designed to intrigue potential readers.

Checklist

A synopsis should include:

1. an explanation of the background
2. the setting in place and time
3. who the main characters are
4. what they are like
5. the theme
6. the main areas of conflict
7. a mention of the major scenes and crises
8. important subplots
9. how the story ends.
   That's the simple part.

Checklist

The synopsis should also convey to an editor:

- the mood
- the style of writing
- any special qualities in your writing, such as humour or lyricism
- whether there is enough plot for the length
- whether the plot progresses
- that you can maintain interest after the first few chapters.

Even if some of the other things in your story or first few chapters are not right, a good professional synopsis might persuade an editor to look at the rest of your novel, to see if it has enough to make working on it a practical option. It could make her encourage you to try again, this time with a better idea of what is wanted by that particular publisher, and a known editor to send it to.

MULTIPLE SUBMISSIONS

This means sending the script simultaneously to more than one publisher. It is being done more now, especially in America, and saves time while waiting for responses, but some publishers refuse to consider it, so check first.

You must say you have sent to others, and if one publisher makes an offer which you accept you must immediately tell the others that the script is sold.

It could save time to send several query letters at once, but make them personal, not a circular which will be binned. You can take up the first favourable response, but the same rules of courtesy apply, you let the others know the position. Publishing is a relatively small world, and gaining a bad reputation is easier than losing one.

How long to wait?

Replies can normally be expected within one to three months, but don't be too impatient. Never pester agents or editors. They don't want authors who might prove difficult.

- 'If this happens, it almost invariably results in an immediate rejection.' (Luigi Bonomi)

Pet hates were:

- 'Prospective writers who want to meet me before I've had a chance to see something they've written.' (Barbara Levy)

- 'Authors who want to meet before I've read their work.' (Carole Blake)

CASE STUDIES: READY TO SUBMIT

Sally feels competitive

'I have no idea which publisher to send it to,' Sally says when she has finished her novel.

'Why not send it in for the Betty Trask awards?' her friend asks. 'You're under 35, and these are for traditional or romantic novels by young authors.'

'That's an idea. And isn't there a Catherine Cookson Prize too? What about the Romantic Novel of the Year?'

'That's for already published novels, but the Catherine Cookson Prize isn't. There are lots of competitions, some might be suitable. The details will be in the yearbooks.'

Sally looks them up, and submits her novel. It doesn't win, but meanwhile she's started another and reads more carefully to see which publishers take her sort of books.

Sally is becoming professional.

Don gets cold feet

'Haven't you sent off the manuscript yet?' Don's wife asks. 'I thought it was all finished last week.'

'I went through it again, and thought of some changes I can make,' Don explains. 'I want to rewrite the first chapter, and every time I look at it I can see other things wrong. I want it to be perfect, so that the agent who was encouraging will accept it, but it seems to be getting worse. I sometimes go back to the first version.'

'You have to stop somewhere. You've probably lost some of the freshness, and can't decide what's good or not. Besides, if you never send it out how can you know whether anyone might buy it? And even when it is bought an editor will almost certainly want to make other changes.'

Don is nervous of getting a rejection, and if he never sends it out that will not happen.

Bridget makes a mistake

Bridget is so pleased to have finished her novel that she wants to send it out right away. Her sister suggests she ought to try and find an agent.

'That's a waste of time, I might as well send it straight to a publisher,' Bridget says, but eventually agrees to try an agent first. She pulls out the old copy of a yearbook she's bought, chooses a couple of names at random, and sends off the manuscript to the first one.

It comes back by return, with a curt note saying that the yearbook states clearly he is not accepting new clients.

Bridget has wasted her time and money because she hasn't bothered to check in a current yearbook.

DISCUSSION POINTS

1. Do you remember discussing English literature at school, and looking beneath the surface for hidden meanings, or discussing clever and apt language? If you reread your own work after a while, do you see in it similar things which you hadn't realised were there?

2. Are you prepared to be patient, trying several agents or publishers, without giving up? How will you select appropriate ones?

3. Would you be willing to do yet more revisions and rewriting if an editor asked you to? What value do you think an editor's suggestions would have?

9
Working with Other Writers

DIFFERENT METHODS

You can work with other writers at a distance, by reading books and magazines. Reading advice manuals or receiving a monthly magazine might be a stimulus to your writing, but the disadvantage is that you get no feedback.

There is feedback with correspondence courses, critical assessment of your work and suggestions for improvement.

The real buzz, however, comes from personal contacts with other writers. This can be done through classes, groups, or special conferences. The majority of writers find that just discussing problems, or even moaning to fellow writers who have the same problems, is a tremendous help in proving you are not alone.

The value of these contacts is felt by many writers.

- 'Encouragement and criticism (is) useful – (I have had) much useful advice.' (Clare Knight)

- 'Draws attention to mistakes, and I find advice helpful, but it can be nit-picking.' (Diana Atkinson)

- 'Mutual support – constructive criticism.' (Zoë March)

BOOKS AND MAGAZINES

Writers' and Artists' Yearbook
This is published annually and has lists of book and magazine publishers, with addresses, special imprints, names of editors, sometimes details of what is wanted such as preliminary letter or first three chapters.

As well as lists of agents there are sections for overseas markets, and information on publishing topics.

The Writer's Handbook
This is a similar annual publication with lists, information on specific publishers and agents, and articles. Both have lists of societies and prizes, and some courses.

Action point
Look at both books before you decide which to buy, since the details about agents or publishers may be more relevant to your needs in one rather than the other. Libraries will have copies, and you may find a secondhand one, but check names, addresses and requirements in the latest edition before sending a manuscript. There are frequent changes of address and personnel.

Magazines
The first four magazines listed below are for beginners, containing hints and factual information. The other two are trade publications read by editors, agents, librarians and booksellers.

Writing Magazine
A monthly magazine available through newsagents. It has interviews with writers and others in the publishing world, articles, details of competitions, a help column, letters page, and advertisements of courses and other services to writers.

Writers News
A monthly subscription magazine, which has market and publishing news. It includes *Writing Magazine*.

Writer's Monthly
Another subscription magazine combining similar aspects to the two above.

Writers' Forum
Similar to the last one, with short fillers and longer articles on all aspects of writing.

The Bookseller
A weekly magazine for the book publishing trade, well worth consulting in libraries, with details about people, publishing houses and the books they publish.

Publishing News
A weekly newspaper with information on books and publishers.

JOINING HOME STUDY COURSES

The magazines advertise correspondence courses. There are several for novelists.

These courses are ideal if you want to work at your own pace, receiving qualified comments on your work. Choose a course where you pay as you go, not one where you will be expected to send a large sum to begin with.

OBTAINING PROFESSIONAL CRITICISM

It may be more constructive, if you have already written a novel, to have it assessed individually. Some agents who charge a reading fee will give a short comment, but for a detailed **critique** you need to pay a specialist.

People who run these services can be practising writers, tutors, publishers' readers, former agents or editors, perhaps working from home while they have young children, or retired.

Criticism services are offered by writing schools. They advertise in the yearbooks and writing magazines. It is sensible if you can to get a personal recommendation, but if you don't know anyone to ask, check the qualifications of the critic and make sure they know the current publishing world. Also ask how much they charge and what they will give you for this.

NETWORKING

This includes gathering knowledge and getting to know people who may impart hot tips about a new agent or publisher long before it's in any magazine.

Finding books and magazines is easy, but how do you go about contacting other writers?

JOINING WRITERS' GROUPS

There are national, regional, local and postal groups, as well as online computer circles on the Internet.

National groups

Mainly for published writers. General ones are the Society of Authors, PEN, and The Writer's Guild, with sub-groups for specialists.

There are organisations for particular genres: the Crime Writers Association which admits published writers, the Romantic Novelists' Association which has a scheme for critiquing the scripts of unpublished members, and the British Fantasy Society which is open to readers as well as writers.

Details are in the yearbooks.

Regional groups

Groups such as Southern Writers, or South West Writers, or the Union of Welsh Writers, are mainly for published writers, but not always. It's worth asking.

Local groups

These vary enormously, from a few people all engaged on the same type of writing to groups with over a hundred members. Most groups meet regularly to read and discuss work, which provides valuable criticism. You need to evaluate the criticism, and know whether it is fair and reliable. The majority of members have published very little, but many published writers and knowledgeable people belong to them, and they are good places to start with. Make sure your aims are the same as theirs. Be wary of unstinting praise: some groups are mutual admiration societies. Others are mainly social.

Groups often have speakers, which is a good way to begin networking. Even if the speaker is not in your own line you can usually pick up hints on methods of work, or research, or simply absorb more information about publishing, all of it adding to your total knowledge.

Libraries will have details of groups in your area.

Postal groups

Postal groups circulate work and add comments before passing it on. If you can't get out to meetings this is the next best way of being in touch with other writers. Some people prefer it, since it allows more time for studying a piece of writing before passing judgement on it.

Start your own

If there is no suitable group near you consider starting your own. Local radios and newspapers are often willing to give free publicity, and nearby libraries and bookshops might put up notices.

Action point
Make a list of possible groups you might join.

ATTENDING COURSES, WORKSHOPS AND WEEKENDS

You could take a degree in writing. Many higher education institutions run full-time courses as well as evening classes, day or weekend schools.

Local education authorities, regional arts councils, writers' groups and commercial organisations run courses. Most are for comparatively small groups and there will be a mixture of talks, discussions and workshop exercises. A few are huge conventions, with many different activities going on at the same time. Lists are in the yearbooks, or can be supplied by libraries and arts councils.

You can often find workshops held in conjunction with literary festivals. Writers come to talk at these festivals and it's a good opportunity of meeting them.

Action point
Begin to collect details of courses advertised, and contact addresses, and decide which would suit you best.

CASE STUDIES – GETTING TOGETHER

Sally makes an assignation
'None of the local writers write novels,' Sally complains. 'Where can I meet other people doing the same thing?'

'What about joining the Romantic Novelists' Association?' her friend who lives some distance away suggests. 'If I join too, we can go to meetings together.'

'We'd meet published writers. Will they let us join?'

'Yes, they have unpublished members too. They have a critique scheme for people like us, once a year. And we can meet editors and agents there. Who knows, one of them might be interested in our manuscripts.'

'Right, let's get details.'

Sally is beginning to network seriously.

Don goes weekending
'This course looks interesting,' Don exclaims. He's reading his

writing magazine. 'It's a whole weekend, and there will be various crime writers and editors there.'

'Plenty of chance to talk to them, I suppose. Why don't you go?' his wife suggests.

'Nice place, too, but I don't suppose I'll have much chance of strolling along the promenade.'

'They have some good shops there. I wonder if I could come as well, and just pay for the hotel? I can do the Christmas shopping while you're at talks.'

They book on the course and his wife complains she doesn't see him between seven in the morning and midnight.

'There's so much to talk about!' he apologises. 'I'm meeting some very useful people, and learning such a lot just by talking in the bar.'

Bridget forms her own group

Bridget's sister's husband died suddenly, and the sisters decide to live together. They move to a different town and there is no suitable writing group, so when they are settled in Bridget decides to form her own.

She talks to the local librarian, and puts notices in libraries and bookshops, sends out press releases to the local newspaper and radio station, and has interviews with both.

The library offers the use of a room for the first meeting, as they have no idea how many people will turn up. 'And you shouldn't advertise your address,' the librarian advises, 'just a telephone number.'

Ten people come to the meeting, three decide they prefer to write poetry, but the rest agree to form a group and spend the evening discussing details.

Bridget has found support and companionship.

DISCUSSION POINTS

1. Read copies of writing magazines and decide if you want to subscribe. Which would be most suitable for you?

2. Read at least two copies of *The Bookseller*, and look for items of use to you, now or in the future.

3. What sort of criticism do you think would be useful to you, and where could you obtain it?

10
Being Published

CONTRACTS, COPYRIGHT AND LEGAL MATTERS

Contracts

These cover **monetary details** such as how much is paid and when, **second rights, author's free copies, remaindering**, and what happens if there is a dispute. Contracts may be a single page or a dozen closely typed pages.

Copyright

Despite recent 'tidying' legislation in the UK the law of **copyright** is extremely complicated. It varies in different countries, and there is a mass of case law which makes trying to interpret the fine details a specialist task. Because of this, infringements of copyright and subsequent court battles can be very expensive.

To give the simplest possible explanation, copyright applies to an author's rights in his work, which exist as soon as he has written it, before publication. This means that other people cannot quote from a piece of work without the author's permission. It applies to lines of songs, or extracts from broadcast scripts. There are exceptions, such as quoting short extracts for purposes of illustration or comment or study, but it would be wise to consult a lawyer before publishing anything you haven't permission to quote. There is no copyright in ideas or titles.

In the UK since January 1996 copyright extends for seventy years after an author's death. A new edition can create a new copyright, so just because an author died over seventy years ago it does not necessarily mean their work is out of copyright and can be quoted freely.

You can give away copyright, and some publishers may ask for this, but it is not a good idea to agree.

Other legal matters
Libel
If something is defamatory and published in a permanent form, such as in writing, it may constitute **libel**. An action for damages can be brought. If you take a living person as a model for your villain, and give him derogatory sayings or actions, you could be in trouble. It's wise to check there isn't a clergyman or accountant with the same name in the town where you set your story, or anyone who might, by great similarity of name, be assumed to be him.

Plagiarism
Ideas, plots and themes are bound to be duplicated since there are a limited number of them, but **plagiarism** consists of a deliberate copying from another person's work and pretending it is your own.

THE PROCESS OF PUBLICATION

It normally takes a year from acceptance of the script to publication, and the author has quite a lot to do still, apart from writing the next novel. There will normally be editorial decisions and consultations, and **proof reading**. The publisher will organise jackets and publicity.

The editor's work
A good editor knows her firm, what it wants, and how to achieve it. Her input is immensely valuable, as she comes to the manuscript with a fresh eye, isn't so deeply enmeshed in the detail as the author is, and can see where changes will improve the whole. A good writer wants to be published and will comply with editorial suggestions, or consider them seriously and perhaps make alternative suggestions to achieve the same objective.

- 'An average manuscript from a new author does need quite a large amount of editing, often two to three sets of revisions need to be carried out.' (Luigi Bonomi)

- 'Varies.' (Judy Piatkus)

- 'Varies dramatically.' (Barbara Boote)

- 'Can vary from no work to many drafts.' (Beverley Cousins)

- 'An author's publisher is, in effect, his/her very first, critical, perhaps over-critical, reader. If something strikes your publisher (who *is* on your side) as not very good, then it may have the same effect on other readers – the buying public, who are not on your side until your book persuades them that they should be.' (Reay Tannahill)

- 'A good editor is worth her weight in gold. Listen to what he/she has to say!' (Joan Hessayon)

The copy-editor's work
After the editor has discussed or suggested changes, the copy-editor will check details.

- 'Most authors can do with a hand over spelling, punctuation, ambiguities, infelicities, inconsistencies.' (Michael Legat)

Then the book will be sent for **typesetting**, or increasingly these days, set from a **computer disk**. **Proofs** will usually come as **double-page spreads**, or **bound** in a paper cover, about six to four months before publication date. The author will need to go through these mainly for typing errors.

BOOK JACKETS

Meanwhile an artist will have been commissioned to design the jacket. You may or may not be asked for suggestions. Some imprints have a common format which is instantly recognisable on the shelves. You may be fortunate to be shown the jacket as it progresses from a drawing to a painting, and asked for comments.

The jackets are used for publicity before the actual books are ready. As well as the cover picture there will be the blurb on the inside front flap which you, the editor, or a special department will be asked to write. This must be designed to tempt the browser into buying or borrowing your book. On a paperback the blurb will be on the outside back cover. Details of the author will usually appear on the back inside flap, and review quotes of this or earlier books somewhere too.

Both librarians and booksellers considered jacket, blurb and title mattered a great deal when they selected books, though readers thought they mattered less. This is probably because readers tended to choose books on the basis of their familiar, favourite authors, or the recommendation of friends. For the new writer's books to be in the library or bookshop, available for choice, their titles and blurbs and jackets need to be good.

Action point
Practise writing intriguing blurbs for books you have read.

PUBLICITY IN MANY GUISES

● 'Publicity is more important than a good review.' (Ralph James)

Other booksellers from both small independents and large chains agreed that advertising influenced sales, though 'word of mouth' (Richard Carr) and 'recommendations and "Book at Bedtime"' (Brian Pattinson) were important.

The final copies will come a month or so before publication, and there is nothing which compares with the thrill of holding your first real book in your hands, unless it's holding your new baby. In many ways a book *is* a baby in that it has taken a long time to produce, and will need constant nurturing for some time yet.

Publishers will have advertised the book, sent out review copies, and tried to get your local papers, magazines and radio stations interested. The launch parties, signings in Harrods, national newspaper reviews, publicity tours and TV chat show appearances happen to very few.

Getting your own publicity
You can do a lot yourself. Some of these suggestions are expensive, but others cost little more than a few postage stamps. What you do must depend on how much you can afford, and whether you feel it is worth your while in terms of present sales, or publicity in the hope of future sales.

Action points: Publicity suggestions
1. Send press releases to your local papers, magazines and radio stations, and try to get them to interview you.

2. Visit local bookshops and try to persuade them to stock and display your books. If they get them, they may be happy for you to sign copies.

3. Offer to talk to local groups. Many organisations are always

eager to know about speakers, especially if you offer to do it just for expenses and a chance to sell your books at the meeting. Most publishers will be happy for you to buy books at a discount for this purpose.

4. Draft leaflets to send to your friends, leave in libraries, or bookshops, or hand out at meetings. Typed and photocopied onto coloured paper they are effective.

5. Throw yourself a launch party, and make sure you have copies to sell to your guests.

6. Have self-adhesive labels printed to put on your correspondence.

7. Have postcards or bookmarks printed, more or less elaborate, to give away.

Reviews

Librarians and booksellers all read reviews, and are influenced by them. Fewer readers read them.

- 'I am also influenced by book programmes on TV and radio (but) to some extent this depends on the reviewer and indeed the style of the review.' (Mary Brackley)

- 'I *am* influenced by reviews, and may borrow/request books from the library accordingly.' (Frances Hawkins)

A minute proportion of published novels is reviewed nationally, so don't expect much publicity from that. You will have more chance of a review in the local press, so cultivate your local journalists.

Regular reviewers do about one book a week, and some have little choice about which books they do. Others have complete freedom to choose. Most told me that they tend to review established authors: 'There are more of them' (F. E. Pardoe), but some will select new writers.

What reviewers liked

- 'Subject matter.' (Rebecca Abrams)

- 'A well written, good plot.' (Sarah Broadhurst)

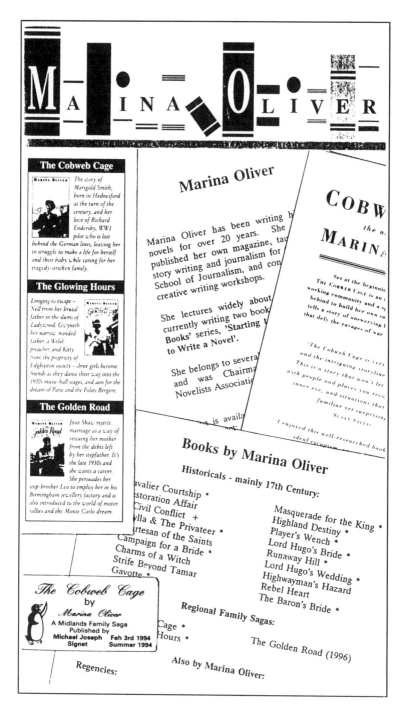

Fig. 9. Publicity aids you can organise.

- 'That it should engage my interest: and fairly quickly!' (F. E. Pardoe)

- 'Good quality in the actual writing, as the lack of it can undermine absolutely every other merit the novel might have.' (Anon)

- 'The writing style, then character.' (Anon)

They disliked:

- 'Reading the same book the author has written before, or borrowed from someone else. Lack of originality.' (F. E. Pardoe)

A reviewer told me that space is so precious that authors should use any contacts they have to get reviews! It's a jungle, but if you can get in, do.

This is depressing for a new writer. A few immensely fortunate ones do get publicity at the start, but for most it's a hard slog. The only way to break in is to produce books regularly, and build up a readership by word of mouth.

ADVANCES, ROYALTIES AND SUBSIDIARY RIGHTS

Advances
Advances are the sums paid before the book is published, or on publication. These will normally be in two parts, one half on signature of contract, one half on publication, but there are variations on this.

Royalties
Royalties are paid once or twice a year, and are normally a percentage of the retail price of the book. Usually the terms are 10 per cent on hardback, less on paperback editions. If sales are high there may be a higher royalty, 12.5 per cent or 15 per cent on sales above a specified quantity. Sometimes with high volume sales at big discounts this may be the percentage of the publisher's receipts, and with 40 per cent or 50 per cent discounts to booksellers this can be far less than authors imagine.

However, the situation has been confused by the breakdown of the **Net Book Agreement**, which means that there is no enforceable selling price.

The advance is set against earnings, so until the book has earned that amount you will receive no more royalties.

Subsidiary rights

Subsidiary rights are the sales for different editions, usually paperback or hardback when to a different publisher, or large print or audio editions. They also cover the sales for translation or to America, to book clubs or for serialisation, condensation or digest, and dramatisation rights for radio, TV or film. There are others, but these are the main ones you are likely to encounter at first.

PUBLIC LENDING RIGHT

This is a payment from a government agency based on the number of times books are borrowed from libraries. There is an upper limit which about a hundred writers reach every year, but the extra income is welcomed by many writers whose books have been published solely in library editions and are rarely available in bookshops unless by special order. It is the responsibility of the author to register in the first place, and to register every new title or edition as it is published.

ALLOWABLE EXPENSES

Keep accounts

Your income, even after publication, will come in just a few times a year, once or twice for the advance, perhaps twice for royalty payments, once for Public Lending Right, and maybe other payments for second rights.

Your expenditure, however, may be daily. Note postage and telephone calls, stationery costs, books and magazines you buy to do with writing or research, travel costs and meals you buy when away from home, and equipment such as a computer or desk. Keep receipts where you have them.

Working out expenses

You can offset allowable expenses against income. Those above, which are directly applicable to your writing, are straightforward, but you may be asked, if you use your computer for other purposes, for example, to make an apportionment of the percentage it is used for writing.

There are other less obvious expenses which may be allowable. If you do research while on holiday, for instance, a proportion of your costs, entry charges into museums, and guide books and maps, could be allowed. You can charge part of the telephone rental charges, and part of your heating and lighting costs. Subscriptions to writing organisations, and travel to their meetings, are allowable as are fees for courses.

INCOME TAX AND VAT

You will be liable for income tax on your 'profit': income minus allowable expenses.

Don't set aside one room for writing, or there could be capital gains tax implications if you sell your house.

You will need to distinguish between running expenses and capital expenditure on equipment and furniture. A proportion of the latter can be set against profits each year. Do consult your tax office, which will send you appropriate leaflets.

At first simple accounts and a sympathetic taxman will be all you need, but as your success builds your tax affairs will become more complicated, and it may be worth employing an accountant. Some firms specialise in advising authors, and the Society of Authors can provide names and addresses.

Value Added Tax

This applies to writers with a higher income, as with other businesses, but by the time you reach this level you will almost certainly have been writing for some time and be employing an accountant.

FINAL TIPS AND WORDS OF ENCOURAGEMENT

Persevere

Very few authors succeed right away. Most spend years before they strike lucky. And luck does sometimes come into it. I asked how long people had been writing before the first acceptance.

- 'About six months. But I'd served a ten-year "apprenticeship" in magazine stories.' (Susan Sallis)

- 'About eight months, ie as long as it took to write the first one.' (Matthew Kneale)

- 'About a year.' (Frederick Nolan)

Income		£	Expenditure		£
Jan	Advance, Bk 4	1,000	Jan	Post	3
				Phone	6
				Paper	20
				Subscriptions	10
					30
					8
				2 days away	100
Feb	PLR	650	Feb	Post	10
				Phone	9
				Padded envps	5
				Typing chair	150
Mar	Fee for talk	50	Mar	Post	5
	Large print advance	400		Phone	7
				Books	30
Apr	Royalties, Bks 1&2	845	Apr	Post	8
				Phone	3
				Env. folders	10

Fig. 10. Simple income and expenditure records.

- 'Four years.' (Joan Hessayon)

- 'Four years.' (Anita Burgh)

- 'Six years.' (Andrew Puckett)

- 'Six years seriously.' (Anne Melville)

- 'Seriously trying to be accepted, about twelve years.' (A. Hulme)

- 'I finished my first novel when I was seventeen. I then wrote four more, very properly unpublished, novels before the first Charles Paris was accepted when I was twenty-nine.' (Simon Brett)

- 'Eighteen years. All my efforts to get a publisher failed. When it happened it was complete chance – a meeting with an agent at a party.' (Sara Banerji)

The writers not yet published had all completed at least three manuscripts, and started several more.

Tips and advice
- 'Read the best before you try to write.' (Judith Murdoch)

- 'Be open to constructive criticism – no one is perfect and you can *always* learn. And never give up.' (Carole Blake)

- 'Persevere, understand that writing is a craft and the more you practise the better you will become. Be prepared to take advice from professional editors. Some promising authors cannot take advice and do not succeed for that reason.' (Judy Piatkus)

- 'A friend once told me: "Remember the value of competence. Forget genius – if you can deliver a piece of work that's on the right subject, and the right length, and meets its deadline and is delivered to the right publisher – then you're already ahead of eighty per cent of professional writers." ' (Simon Brett)

- 'Be aware of the market but don't be afraid to be original.' (Hilary Johnson)

- 'Persevere if you believe in yourself.' (Jane Morpeth)

- 'If a busy editor has taken time to write a critique (with a rejection slip) it's because she thinks there's something there worth criticising. If she asks to see some more work, send some.' (Ann Hulme)

- 'Sometimes you'll have bad days and will think you'll be writing rubbish. Often you'll be right. But keep going and you may just end up with something that's grown and fused into something far better than you would ever have believed on those bad days.' (Matthew Kneale)

- 'Keep writing – keep launching those messages in bottles, be patient, your time will come, even if it's 200 years in the future when they discover your genius, and always read.' (Philip Pullman)

- 'Publishers are always looking for the writer with a new idea or a fresh voice. Don't be afraid to follow your own star – it's always better than following someone else's.' (Frederick Nolan)

- 'Don't give up. Cultivate a sense of humour. Accept that life is Not Fair for most people, and Especially Not Fair for writers.' (Andrew Puckett)

- 'Most important, relax and enjoy writing or else it will show.' (Anita Burgh)

CASE STUDIES: PUBLICATION ISN'T THE END OF IT

Sally can't understand the contract

Sally has sold her third attempt at a novel. She is thrilled, until the contract comes and then the vast amount of detail frightens her.

'I don't understand more than half the words in this.'

'Perhaps you should let a solicitor see it.'

'But will he understand publishing terms? And will he know what's fair, or normal? Some parts look as though I don't have any say in anything at all!'

'Then ask an agent.'

'None of them wanted me before.'

'Surely they will now you've proved you can do it.'

Sally approaches a new agent, who reads her novel and agrees to represent her. She advises Sally on the contract, suggesting changes which the publisher agrees.

Sally is on the way to publication.

Don doesn't like being edited

'They want me to change everything!' Don says when he reads the editor's letter. 'Why did they offer to buy the novel if they want to make all these changes?'

'Let me see,' his wife says, and takes the letter. 'It doesn't look too bad. One or two things look quite sensible suggestions, which you hadn't thought of. Will you agree?'

'I don't like them changing *my* work.'

'If you don't agree, they might turn it down. You haven't had a contract yet. And you've been rejected by half a dozen other publishers. It might be difficult to find anyone else.'

He sighs. 'I suppose so. I don't want to get a reputation for being difficult.'

Don is facing reality.

Bridget does her own publicity

'You can send out press releases like you did for the writers' group,' Bridget's sister says when publication day comes near. 'I saw a book on how to do your own PR in the bookshop last week.'

'The publisher will do that. They asked me for local newspaper addresses.'

'But newspapers must have lots of letters and press releases from big firms. Local newspapers want the personal angle. I bet they'll take more notice of one from you. And you can send them to the old town as well as here.'

Bridget begins to get enthusiastic. 'I'll go and visit all the local bookshops too, and the libraries. And perhaps Jane will get the old group to invite me to give a talk.'

'And the women's groups. They always have problems finding speakers.'

Bridget is on the verge of a speaking career too.

DISCUSSION POINTS

1. Look at some book jackets and decide which are most effective, and why.

2. What sort of personal publicity do you feel able to do?

3. How well do you understand contracts and taxation leaflets? Do you need professional help with these before you get into a muddle?

Appendix 1
Sources of Quotes

AGENTS

Carole Blake. Joint Managing Director, Blake Friedman,Literary, TV and Film Agency Ltd.

Barbara Levy. Sole Proprietor, Barbara Levy Literary Agency.

Laura Longrigg. Literary Agent, Jennifer Kavanah Agency.

Dorothy Lumley. Proprietor, Dorian Literary Agency.

Sarah Molloy. Director, A. M. Heath & Co Ltd.

Judith Murdoch. Proprietor, Judith Murdoch Literary Agency.

Caroline Sheldon. Proprietor, Caroline Sheldon Literary Agency.

Bob Tanner. Managing Director, International Scripts.

BOOKSELLERS

Richard Carr. Customer Service Manager, WH Smith's, High Wycombe.

Ralph James. Director, James Redshaw Ltd, Lichfield.

Brian Pattinson. Owner of several bookshops in Oxfordshire.

EDITORS

Diane Allen. Rights and Acquisitions Manager, Magna Large Print Books.

Jill Black. Former Editorial Director, The Bodley Head. Administrator for the Georgette Heyer and the Catherine Cookson Prizes.

Luigi Bonomi. Editorial Director, Signet (Penguin Books Ltd).

Barbara Boote. Editorial Director, Little, Brown and Company (UK) Ltd.

Beverley Cousins. Senior Editor. Macmillan Publishers Ltd

Elizabeth Johnson. Senior Editor, Harlequin Mills and Boon Ltd.

Hilary Johnson. Freelance Editor.

Michael Legat. Ex-Editorial Director, and author of several writers' guides.

Jane Morpeth. Publishing Director (Fiction), Headline.
Judy Piatkus. Managing Director, Piatkus Books.
Deborah Smith. Managing Editor, Severn House Publishers.
Richenda Todd. Senior Editor, Michael Joseph.

LIBRARIANS

Anne Ambler. Oxfordshire.
Christine Budworth. District Librarian, Cannock.
Tracy Long. Library Manager, Solihull.
Sue Richardson. Library Manager, Solihull.
Lynn Sanders. Library Supervisor, Walsall.
Mary Wilson. Holt Jackson Book Co.

NOVELISTS – PUBLISHED

Sara Banerji. Author of several highly acclaimed novels set in India.
Simon Brett. Radio and TV script writer, broadcaster, author of crime novels.
Anita Burgh. Best-selling author of both historical and modern books.
Joan Hessayon. Author of several historicalsm set in England and America.
Ann Hulme. Author of historicals as Ann Hulme, and more recently crime novels as Ann Granger.
Matthew Kneale. Runner-up for the Betty Trask Award, winner of both the Somerset Maugham Award and John Llewellyn Rhys Memorial Award.
Anne Melville. Writes under several pseudonyms, adult and children's fiction, and short stories. Winner (as Anne Betteridge) of the Romantic Novel of the Year Award (1967) with *The Truth Game*.
Haydn Middleton. Author of best-selling historical and fantasy novels.
Frederick Nolan. Novelist, script-writer, former reviewer and workshop leader.
Andrew Puckett. Has written several crime novels and teaches writing classes.
Philip Pullman. Author of novels for children and young adults, historical and fantasy.
Susan Sallis. Best-selling author of many family sagas.
Reay Tannahill. Winner of the Romantic Novel of the Year Award

(1990) with *Passing Glory*, has also written acclaimed non-fiction books.

NOVELISTS – UNPUBLISHED

Diana Atkinson
Clare Knight
Zoë March

READERS

Joan Beard
Valerie Bennett
Mary Brackley
Nancy Brazier
Hanna Bridgeman
Jo Crocker
Molly Frearson
Frances Hawkins
Sylvia Parker
Judy Phillips
Jill Rundle

REVIEWERS

Rebecca Abrams. Freelance reviewer of both fiction and non-fiction for *The Guardian*, also author of non-fiction books, and journalist.
Sarah Broadhurst. Freelance reviewer for *The Bookseller*, several regional papers, *Woman's Journal* and radio.
F.E. Pardoe. Retired as Head of Communication Studies at Birmingham Polytechnic (now the University of Central England). Reviews mainly crime for *The Birmingham Post*.

Appendix 2
List of Publishers of Novels

KEY TO TYPES OF FICTION PUBLISHED

A – adventure, thrillers   C – crime, mystery, suspense
G – general   H – historical
L – literary   R – romantic
S – science fiction, fantasy   O – other

PUBLISHERS

Allison & Busby (**C, G, O**) 179 King's Cross Road, London WC1X 9BZ. Tel: (0171) 833 1042. Fax: (0171) 833 1044.

Bellew Publishing Co Ltd (**C, G, H**) The Nightingale Centre, 8 Balham Hill, London SW12 9EA. Tel: (0181) 673 5611. Fax: (0181) 675 2142.

Black Ace Books (**G, H, L**) Ellemford Farmhouse, Duns, Berwickshire TD11 3SG. Tel: (01361) 890 370. Fax: (01361) 890 287.

Blake Publishing (**A, C, G, S**) 3 Bramber Court, 2 Bramber Road, London W14 9PB. Tel: (0171) 381 0666. Fax: (0171) 381 6868.

Bloomsbury (**A, C, G, L**) 2 Soho Square, London W1V 6HB. Tel: (0171) 494 2111. Fax: (0171) 434 0151.

Marion Boyars Publishers Ltd (**G, H, L, O**) 24 Lacy Road, London SW15 1NL. Tel: (0181) 788 952. Fax: (0181) 789 8122.

Calder Publications Ltd (**L**) 179 King's Cross Road, London WC1X 9BZ. Tel: (0171) 833 1300.

Canongate Books Ltd (**G, H, L**) 14 High Street, Edinburgh EH1 1TE. Tel: (0131) 557 5111. Fax: (0131) 557 5211.

Cassell (Victor Gollancz) (**C, S**) Wellington House, 125 Strand, London WC2R 0BB. Tel: (0171) 420 5555. Fax: (0171) 240 7261.

Robin Clark Ltd (**H**) 27 Goodge Street, London W1P 1FD. Tel: (0171) 636 3992. Fax: (0171) 637 1866.

Richard Cohen Books (**A, C, O, G, H**) Basement Offices, 7

Manchester Square, London W1M 5RE. Tel: (0171) 935 2099. Fax: (0171) 935 2199.

Constable & Co Ltd (**C, G, H, L**) 3 The Lanchesters, 162 Fulham Palace Road, London W6 9ER. Tel: (0181) 741 3663. Fax: (0181) 748 7562.

Creation Books (**O**) 83 Clerkenwell Road, London EC1M 5RJ. Tel: (0171) 430 9878. Fax: (0171) 242 5527.

Dedalus Ltd (**O, L**) 24 St Judith's Lane, Sawtry, Cambs PE17 5XE. Tel and Fax: (01487) 832 382.

Andre Deutsch Ltd (**C, G, H, L**) 105–106 Great Russell Street, London WC1B 3LJ. Tel: (0171) 580 2746. Fax: (0171) 631 3253.

Gerald Duckworth & Co Ltd (**G**) 48 Hoxton Square, London N1 6PB. Tel: (0171) 729 5986. Fax: (0171) 729 0015.

Faber & Faber Ltd (**C, G, L, O**) 3 Queen Square, London WC1N 3AU. Tel: (0171) 465 0045. Fax: (0171) 465 0034.

Fourth Estate Ltd (**A, C, G, H, L, O**) 6 Salem Road, London W2 4BU. Tel: (0171) 727 8993. Fax: (0171) 792 3176.

Gairm Publications (**A, C, G, L**) 29 Waterloo Street, Glasgow G2 6BZ. Tel and Fax: (0141) 221 1971.

Gay Men's Press, G. M. P. Publishers Ltd (**O**) PO Box 247, London N6 4BW. Tel: (0181) 341 7818. Fax: (0181) 341 7467.

Granta Publications Ltd (**G**) 2/3 Hanover Yard, Noel Road, London N1 8BE. Tel: (0171) 704 9776. Fax: (0171) 704 0474.

Robert Hale Ltd (**G, H, R, O**) Clerkenwell House, 45–47 Clerkenwell Green, London WC1R 0HT. Tel: (0171) 251 2661. Fax: (0171) 490 4958.

Harlequin Mills & Boon (Mills and Boon **R**, Mira **R**, Silhouette **R**) Eton House, 18–24 Paradise Road, Richmond, Surrey TW9 1SR. Tel: (0181) 948 0444. Fax: (0181) 940 5899.

HarperCollins (**A, C, G, H, L, R, S**) (Collins **C**, Flamingo **L**) 77–85 Fulham Palace Road, Hammersmith, London W6 8JB. Tel: (0181) 741 7070. Fax: (0181) 307 4440.

Hodder Headline (**A, C, G, H, L, S, R**) (Coronet **A, C, R, S**, Delta **O**, Liaison **O**, New English Library **A, C, S**, Sceptre **A, C, G, H, L**) 338 Euston Road, London NW1 3BH. Tel: (0171) 873 6000. Fax: (0171) 873 6024.

Impact Books Ltd (**L**) Axe & Bottle Court, 70 Newcomen Street, London SE1 1YT. Tel: (0171) 403 3541. Fax: (0171) 407 6437.

Karnack House (**L**) 300 Westbourne Park Road, London W11 1EH. Tel and Fax: (0171) 221 6490.

Little, Brown & Company (**A, C, G, H, R, S**) (Abacus L, Orbit S, Warner **A, C, G, H, O, R**, Virago **A, C, G, H, L, O**) Brettenham

House, Lancaster Place, London WC2E 7EN. Tel: (0171) 911
8000. Fax: (0171) 911 8100.

Macmillan Publishers Ltd (C, G, L, R) (Pan, A, C, G, H, L, R, S,
Picador L) 25 Eccleston Place, London SW1W 9NF. Tel: (0171)
881 8000.

Mainstream Publishing Co (Edinburgh) Ltd (G, H, L) 7 Albany
Street, Edinburgh EH1 3UG. Tel: (0131) 557 2959. Fax: (0131)
556 8720.

The Orion Publishing Group Ltd (A, C, G, H, L, R, S) Chapman
O, Millenium S, Phoenix House L) Orion House, 5 Upper St
Martin's Lane, London WC2H 9EA. Tel: (0171) 240 3444. Fax:
(0171) 240 4822.

Peter Owen Ltd (G, H, L, O) 73 Kenway Road, London SW5 0RE.
Tel: (0171) 373 5628. Fax: (0171) 373 6760.

Penguin Books Ltd (Hamish Hamilton C, G, L, O, Signet G, R, S,
Viking, C, G, L Michael Joseph A, C, H, R) 27 Wrights Lane,
London W8 5TZ. Tel: (0171) 416 3000. Fax: (0171) 416 3099.

Piatkus Books (A, C, G, H, R) 5 Windmill Street, London W1P
1HF. Tel: (0171) 631 0710. Fax: (0171) 436 7137.

Quartet Books Ltd (G) 27–29 Goodge Street, London W1P 1FD.
Tel: (0171) 636 3992. Fax: (0171) 637 1866.

Rampant Horse Ltd (A, C, G, H, L) 140 Whitehall Road, Norwich,
Norfolk NR2 3EW. Tel: (01603) 665 843. Fax: (01603) 661 589.

Random House UK Ltd (A, C, G, H, L, R, S) Arrow C, S, Cape G,
H, L Chatto A, C, G, L Century G, L, R, Hutchinson A, C, G, H,
L, Legend S) Random House, 20 Vauxhall Bridge Road,
London SW1V 2SA. Tel: (0171) 973 9000. Fax: (0171) 233 608.

Reed International Books (currently being split up and imprints
sold.) (Heinemann A, C, G, H, L, R, Mandarin G, Methuen G,
L, Minerva L, Secker & Warburg, G, L, Sinclair Stephenson A,
C, G, H, L) Michelin House, 81 Fulham Road, London SW3
6RB. Tel: (0171) 581 9393. Fax: (0171) 225 9424.

Robinson Publishing Ltd (O, R, S) 7 Kensington Church Court,
London W8 4SP. Tel: (0171) 938 3830. Fax: (0171) 938 4214.

Seren Books (G) First Floor, 2 Wyndham Street, Bridgend, Mid
Glamorgan CF31 1EF. Tel: (01656) 767 834.

Serif (L, O) 47 Strahan Road, London E3 5DA. Tel and Fax: (0181)
981 3990.

Serpent's Tail (C, G, L, O) 4 Blackstock Mews, London N4 2BT.
Tel: (0171) 354 1949. Fax: (0171) 704 6467.

Severn House Publishers (A, C, R, S) 9–15 High Street, Sutton,
Surrey SM1 1DF. Tel: (0181) 770 3930. Fax: (0181) 770 3850.

Simon & Schuster (**A, G, H**) (Pocket Books **G**) West Garden Place, Kendal Street, London W2 2AQ. Tel: (0171) 724 7577. Fax: (0171) 402 0639.

Skoob Books Publishing Ltd (**L**) 25 Lowman Road, London N7 6DD. Tel and Fax: (0171) 609 0699.

Souvenir Press Ltd (**A, C, G, H, L**) 43 Great Russell Street, London WC1B 3PA. Tel: (0171) 580 9307. Fax: (0171) 580 5064.

Stride Publications (**O**) 11 Sylvan Road, Exeter, Deveon EX4 6EW.

Titan Books Ltd (**C, S, O**) (Eros Plus **O**) 42-44 Dolben Street, London SE1 0UP. Tel: (0171) 620 0200. Fax: (0171) 620 0032.

Transworld Publishers Ltd (Bantam **A, C, G, H, L, R, S, O**, Black Swan **A, C, G, H, L, R, S**, Corgi **A, C, G, L, R, S, O**, Doubleday **A, G, H, L, R**) 61–63 Uxbridge Road, London W5 5SA. Tel: (0181) 579 2652. Fax: (0181) 579 5479.

Virgin Publishing Ltd (Black Lace **O**, Nexus **O**) 332 Ladbroke Grove, London W10 5AH. Tel: (0181) 968 7554. Fax: (0181) 968 0929.

The Women's Press (**A, L, S, O**) 34 Great Sutton Street, London EC1V 0DX. Tel: (0171) 251 3007. Fax: (0171) 608 1938.

Yorkshire Art Circus (**O**) School Lane, Glass Houghton, Castleford, West Yorkshire WF10 4QH. Tel: (01977) 50 401. Fax: (01977) 512 819.

Glossary

Acceptance. An offer to publish the manuscript.

Advance. Money given to an author by a publisher on signing a contract to write a book and/or on delivery of script and publication of that book.

Agent. A person or company that acts on an author's behalf, selling the author's work and negotiating fees. Agents take a percentage of authors' earnings.

aka. also known as.

Allowable expenses. Those expenses on machinery, equipment and essential requirements an author has in order to work, which can be offset against income before income tax is charged.

Angle. The way something is shown, which might be serious or funny, mysterious or straightforward, or the point of view it is written from.

Auctions. An agent will invite several publishers to bid for a script by a certain deadline. This happens with a few very important works.

Blockbuster. A large book of fiction, often aimed at the holiday market.

Blurb. A summary of the book which is printed on the back cover or on the first page of a book, and designed to attract readers.

Book jacket. The outer cover of the book, usually with an illustration.

Cast. The characters in your novel.

Category fiction. Books/fiction of a particular type, eg romance or science fiction, which are published as a regular series and have similarities within the series such as length, style and conventions.

Characters. The people who feature in your novel.

Cliffhanger. An exciting, unresolved situation at the end of a scene or chapter.

Competition. Where a prize is given for a novel, either published or in script form.

Conflict. Some disagreement, aims which are incompatible.

Contents. The list at the start of a book/magazine which lists the subjects covered and/or chapter headings and page numbers.

Continuity. Keeping details consistent from scene to scene.

Contract. The terms agreed by author and publisher, covering such matters as payment, publication, ownership of second rights and proportions of earnings allocated under these.

Copy. A piece of writing sent to a publisher.

Copy-editing. Checking details and altering a writer's work for the house style of the publisher.

Copyright. The legal rights an author/publisher has over their work, so that no one can copy all or part of the work without the author's or publisher's permission.

Courses. Lectures and exercises, by post or in person, on the art and various aspects of writing.

Cover sheet. The first page of a manuscript giving title, author, author's address and telephone number, and wordage.

Creative writing classes/courses. Often run by local authorities or educational institutions, they may be weekly sessions, day or weekend or longer.

Criticism. A detailed appraisal of a piece of writing.

Critique group. A group of writers who meet to criticise (hopefully constructively) others' work. Groups usually comprise amateur writers, but published writers do join.

Deadline. The date by which a writer aims to complete or submit a script.

Description. Portraying scenes in words.

Deus ex machina. Literally the 'God from the machine', an unexpected event which solves an apparently impossible situation.

Dialect. The words peculiar to one region or area of a country.

Dialogue. Conversation, or the words spoken by characters.

Double spacing. Lines typed to give approximately three lines per inch on a manuscript (single spacing gives six).

Draft. A version of a manuscript, usually the first thoughts.

Edition. A book may be published in different formats, each one is a separate edition.

Editor. The person who commissions writers for books/articles/plays and who sees the project through to the final printing and distribution.

Editing. Checking on accuracy, consistency, relevance, structure, and generally preparing a piece of writing for publication.

Enquiry letter. Letter to the editor outlining what an author has written, how long it is and why it might be of interest to the publisher.

Exposition. An explanation of events, feelings or actions in the novel.

Flashback. Portrayal of a scene from the past as if it is taking place now.

Flash forward. Putting in a scene from the future, or a brief foretelling of what is still to come.

Font. A style and size of type, eg *italic* 10.

Genre. A type of book, eg crime, fantasy, historical, literary, romantic, saga, science fiction, western.

Grammar. Rules applying to words and their relationships to one another.

Hardback. Where the cover of the book is stiff.

Hook. The means by which a writer obtains the reader's attention and interest.

House style. Every publisher/magazine will have certain ways of writing things, for example standardising on spellings such as the use of 'ise' instead of 'ize' at the end of words like criticise.

Internet. A link, via a computer and telephone, to other computers for correspondence, information, or exchange of ideas.

Jeopardy. A danger or peril which threatens characters. A sub-genre of romantic fiction is the 'woman in jeopardy'.

Large print. Editions of a book in a big typeface, intended to make reading easier for people with eyesight problems.

Layout. The way the writing is set out on the page, with margins, line spacing, headings.

Libel. A false, damaging statement published in permanent form.

Manuscript/script/typescript. An author's typed/word processed piece of work.

Market. Any place where a writer's work may be sold.

Modifiers. Words which qualify, change or restrict others.

Moral rights. The rights of 'paternity', *ie* having one's authorship recognised, and of integrity, *ie* not having the work changed in a 'derogatory' manner. These rights have to be asserted in writing by the author.

Multiple submissions. Sending work to more than one publisher at a time.

Narrative. The telling of a story.

Networking. Forming connections with other people.

Online. A connection to another computer or a service.

Outline. A very brief summary of a piece of work.

Pace. The speed of progress, whether fast or slow, smooth or jerky, of a piece of writing.

Padding. Inserting irrelevant detail.

Page proofs. Typeset manuscripts in page layout.

Paperback. A book the cover of which is flexible card or thick paper.

Partials. Part of a book which the publisher likes to see, in order to judge whether to read the rest with a view to publication. It is normally the first three chapters or fifty pages.

Phonetics. Writing sounds, especially of regional or foreign accents, using one symbol for each sound rather than the conventional spelling. Miss could be mees or mizz.

Plagiarism. Deliberately to copy another writer's ideas such as plot and characters and use them as your own.

Plot. A series of happenings connected by cause and effect.

Polishing. Checking a manuscript to make final changes and corrections.

Presentation. The way in which a manuscript is shown to an editor.

Printer. 1) The machine which produces, on paper, documents stored in a computer. There are different types using different processes. 2) The person or firm which typesets books and produces copies.

Program. The system by which a computer receives and deals with data.

Proofreading. Final check of galleys or page proofs for typos, spelling mistakes, missing text and so on.

Proofs. Typeset article/book which is corrected for printing.

Proof marks. The symbols used to indicate changes needed.

Proposal. Detailed outline of a project, together with a synopsis.

Protagonist. One of the leading characters.

Pseudonym. A name used by an author which is not his own, a pen name.

Publicity. Spreading information by various means, the media or personally.

Public Lending Right. Money an author gets each time her book is borrowed from a library. The author must register each new edition on publication or before the end of June each year to receive payment the following February.

Publisher's reader. Someone who reads and assesses manuscripts, and passes on suitable ones for final editorial decision on buying.

Pulping. When books/magazines are sent back to the publisher/ distributor because they are not bought, some are destroyed by reducing them to pulp which then goes to make paper.

Punctuation. Symbols used to make the written words clear and understandable.

Rejections. When an agent or publisher declines to handle or buy a manuscript. There are many reasons for rejection apart from the quality of the work.

Remainders. The books that are left after sales have fallen off are remaindered – offered to the author at a cheap rate and to cheap book shops.

Research. Discovering and verifying facts which may be used in or as background for the novel.

Review. A report, usually in the media, assessing a book.

Revising. Checking a piece of writing and making changes in it, improving it, and making sure the facts are accurate.

Rewriting. Changing a piece of writing, sometimes radically, sometimes with only minor alterations.

Rights. Legal rights of an author in terms of the sale of a piece of work.

Royalties. A percentage of the selling price of a book that goes to the author after publication, based on the numbers sold or the monies received.

Second rights. Editions of a book or article after the first publication, eg paperback, large print, translation, syndication, extracts, anthologies, adaptations for radio or TV or film.

Shape. The form and pattern of the novel

Slush pile. The term used for unsolicited manuscripts received.

Softback. See paperback.

Solicited script. Work an editor has asked to see.

Spread. Two pages facing one another in a book or magazine.

Subplot. A minor, subsidiary plot in a novel.

Suspense. Uncertainty about the outcome.

Submissions. The manuscripts sent to editors for consideration, in the hope of acceptance.

Summary. A three- or four-line outline of what a piece of writing is all about.

Synonym. A word with the same or a similar meaning as another word.

Synopsis. A detailed summary of a novel, giving all important facts about the plot and characters.

Target. Aim.

Theme. A subject of a novel, often an abstract quality.

Thesaurus. A book which gives alternative words of the same or similar meaning, and where concepts are grouped.

Title page. Cover sheet of manuscript.

Trade paperback. A book with a flexible cover, but usually of a larger format and higher price than the conventional paperback.

Turning point. A crisis or time when some decision is made or resolution achieved.

Typeface. The style of the typed characters. There are many different typefaces, publishers will use different ones for different projects.

Typos. Typing errors on the manuscript or galleys.

Typesetting. Putting a piece of writing into the typeface, size and in the appropriate space that the publisher uses.

Unsolicited. Work sent on spec to an agent or editor.

VAT. Value Added Tax, imposed on almost all purchases, which can be reclaimed by persons registered under the scheme.

Viewpoint. The character through whose eyes the action is seen or described.

Voice. The particular individual style of a writer.

White space. The empty space at the ends of short lines and chapters.

Wordage. The approximate number of words in a manuscript, calculated by multiplying the average number per line by the lines in a page and the total pages.

Word processing. Using a computer in order to type work, and then being able to manipulate the information by inserting, deleting, moving text, changing the layout and many more processes.

Writer's block. When a writer cannot continue, through lack of ideas or motivation, exhaustion, or psychological difficulties.

Yearbook. A reference book published annually, such as *The Writers' and Artists' Yearbook* **or** *The Writer's Handbook.*

Useful Addresses

WRITING COURSES

Correspondence colleges

Correspondence colleges provide both general and specific courses.

The London School of Journalism, 22 Upbrook Mews, Bayswater, London W2 3HG. Tel: (0171) 706 3536. Fax: (0171) 706 3780.

The Writer's Bureau, Sevendale House, 7 Dale Street, Manchester M1 1JB. Tel: (01612) 282 362.

Writers News Home Study Division, PO Box 4, Nairn IV12 4HU.

The Writing School, 29 Turnpike Lane, London N8 0EP. Tel: (0181) 342 8980.

Short courses

Creative writing short courses, usually residential, are held in many places including the following venues. As programmes change every year, contact the course organisers for details.

Alston Hall, Longridge, Preston PR3 3BP. Tel: (01772) 784 661. Fax: (01772) 785 835.

The Arvon Foundation, Lumb Bank, Heptonstall, Hebden Bridge, West Yorks HX7 6DF. Tel: (01422) 843 714.

The Arvon Foundation, Moniack Mhor, Teavarran, Kiltarlity, Beauly, Inverness-shire IV4 7HT. Tel: (01463) 74675.

The Arvon Foundtion, Totleigh Barton, Sheepwash, Beaworthy, Devon EX21 5NS. Tel: (01409) 23338.

University of Birmingham School of Continuing Studies, Edgbaston, Birmingham B15 2TT. Tel: (01214) 145 615. Fax: (01214) 145 619.

Burton Manor College, Burton, South Wirral, Cheshire L64 5SJ. Tel: (01513) 365 172. Fax: (01513) 366 586.

University of Cambridge Board of Continuing Education, Madingley Hall, Madingley, Cambridge CB3 8AQ. Tel: (01954) 210 636. Fax: (01954) 210 677.

The City Literary Institute, Room 24, Stukely Street, London WC2B 5LJ. Tel: (0171) 430 0542. Fax: (0171) 405 3347.

Creative Space, Lunga Mill, Ardfern, Argyle, PA31 8QR. Tel: (01852) 5526.

Dillington House, Ilminster, Somerset TA19 9DT. Tel: (01460) 52427. Fax: (01460) 52433.

The Earnley Concourse, Earnley, Chichester, Sussex PO20 7JL. Tel: (01243) 670 392. Fax: (01243) 670 832.

University of Edinburgh Centre for Continuing Education, 11 Buccleuch Place, Edinburgh EH8 9LW. Tel: (01316) 504 400. Fax: (01316) 676 097.

Fen Farm, Fen Road, Blo Norton, Near Diss, Norfolk IP22 2JH.

Knuston Hall Residential Colllege, Irchester, Wellingborough, Northamptonshire NN9 7EU. Tel: (01933) 312 104. Fax: (01933) 57596.

Lancaster University Summer Programme Office, The Storey Institute, Lancaster LA1 1TH. Tel: (01524) 382 118. Fax: (01524) 849 499.

Malham Tarn Field Centre, Settle, North Yorkshire BD24 9PU. Tel: (01279) 830 331.

Maryland College, Woburn, Milton Keynes MK17 9JD. Tel: (01525) 290 688.

Missenden Abbey, Great Missenden, Bucks HP16 0BD. Tel: (01494) 890 295.

New Venture Holidays, 18 Old Chester Road, Bebington, Wirral, Merseyside L63 7LQ. Tel: (01516) 452 532.

The Old Rectory, Fittleworth, Pulborough, West Sussex RH20 1HU. Tel: (01798) 82306.

The Poet's House, 80 Portmuck Road, Portmuck, Islandmagee, County Antrim BT40 3TP, Northern Ireland. Tel: (01960) 382 646.

Rewley House, 1 Wellington Square, Oxford OX1 2JA. Tel: (01865) 270 396. Fax: (01865) 270 309.

St Andrews University Holidays, 66 North Street, St Andrews KY16 9AH. Tel: (01334) 62202.

University of Southampton Department of Adult Education, Highfield, Southampton SO9 5NH. Tel: (01703) 593 469. Fax: (01703) 677 642.

Suffolk College, Rope Walk, Ipswich IP4 1LT. Tel: (01473) 255 885. Fax: (01473) 230 054.

Summer Academy, University of Kent, Canterbury CT2 7NX. Tel: (01227) 470 402. Fax: (01227) 784 338.

Swanwick Writers' Summer School, The New Vicarage, Parsons Street, Woodford Halse, Daventry, Northants NN11 3RE. Tel: (01327) 61477.

The Taliesin Trust, Ty Newydd, Llanystumdwy, Criccieth LL52 0LW. Tel: (01766) 522 811. Fax: (01766) 523 095.

Trefechan Arts Centre, Pennant Melangell, Nr LLangynog, Powys SY10 0EU. Tel: (01691) 74346.

Urchfont Manor College, Urchfont, Nr Devizes, Wiltshire SN10 4RG. Tel: (01380) 840 495. Fax: (01380) 840 005.

West Dean College, West Dean, Chichester, West Sussex, PO18 0QZ. Tel: (01243) 811 301. Fax: (01243) 811 343.

Westham House Adult Residential College, Barford, Warwick CV35 8DP. Tel: (01926) 624 206. Fax: (01926) 624 960.

Higher education and professional courses

BA, MA, and Media Studies. Lists of the courses run by universities and other specialist bodies can be found in *The Writers' and Artists' Yearbook*.

PROFESSIONAL ASSOCIATIONS

Once you are published there are many specialist associations. Addresses or contacts can be found in writers' handbooks. Subscriptions sometimes vary for different categories of members, check before you send. There may also be separate charges for meetings.

Denotes associations that are open to unpublished writers.

The British Fantasy Society,* 2 Harwood Street, Heaton Norris, Stockport, Cheshire SK4 1JJ. Tel: (01614) 765 368. For everyone interested in fantasy/horror. Publishes *British Fantasy Newsletter*, plus other annual booklets. Annual convention and awards. Annual subscription £15.

The British Science Fiction Association Ltd,* 52 Woodhill Drive, Grove, Oxon OX12 0DF. For anyone interested in science fiction. Publishes *Matrix, Focus* and *Vector* magazines. Annual subscription £12.

Fellowship of Christian Writers,* Shee-Dy-Vea, 151A Bedford Road, Marston Moretaine, Bedford MK43 0LD. Tel: (01234) 767 470. Manuscript criticism service and network of writers' groups available.

The Friends of the Arvon Foundation,* 6 Church Street, Darfield, Yorkshire S73 9LG. Publishes newsletter. Annual subscription £5.

London Writers' Circle,* Flat D, 49 Christchurch Street, London SW3 4AS. Meetings and workshops.

PEN International, for developing friendship and protecting freedom of speech. English PEN Centre, 7 Dilke Strret, London SW3 4JE. Tel: (0171) 352 6303. Fax: (0171) 351 0220. Annual subscription (London) £30, (country and overseas) £25.

The Penman Club,* 185 Daws Heath Road, Benfleet, Essex SS7 2TF. Tel: (01702) 557 431. Offers advice and criticism. Annual subscription £15 for first year, £8.25 for subsequent years.

The Romantic Novelists' Association,* 5 St Agnes Gate, Wendover, Bucks HP22 6DP. Tel: (01296) 623 260. Offers criticism for unpublished members, plus meetings. Publishes newsletter. Annual subscription £25 plus £30 reading fee.

The Scottish Association of Writers,* 36 Cloan Crescent, Bishopbriggs, Glasgow G64 2HL. Tel: (0141) 772 5604. Organises conferences, competitions and workshops for member clubs.

Society of Authors, 84 Drayton Gardens, London SW10 9SB. Tel: (0171) 373 6642. Fax: (0171) 373 5768. For professional writers. Publishes quarterly journal *The Author*, plus guides on subjects like tax. Meetings and social events. Annual subscription £65.

Society of Women Writers and Journalists,* 110 Whitehall Road, Chingford, London E4 6DW. Tel: (0181) 529 0886. Meetings and advice services. Publishes quarterly newsletter. Annual subscription London £21, country £18.

Women Writers' Network,* c/o 23 Prospect Road, London NW2 2JU. Tel: (0171) 794 5861. Monthly London meetings. Publishes newsletter and directory. Annual subscription £25.

Writers' Guild of Great Britain, 430 Edgware Road, London W2 1EH. Tel: (0171) 723 8074. Fax: (0171) 706 2413. Trade union for writers.

OTHER USEFUL ADDRESSES

Arts Council of England, 14 Great Peter Street, London SW1P 3NQ. Tel: (0171) 333 0100. Fax: (0171) 973 6590.

Welsh Arts Council, 9 Museum Place, Cardiff CF1 3NX. Tel: (01222) 394 711. Fax: (01222) 221 447.

Scottish Arts Council, 12 Manor Place, Edinburgh EH3 7DD. Tel: (01312) 266 051.

N. Ireland Arts Council, 185 Stranmillis Road, Belfast BT9 5DU. Tel: (01232) 381 591. Fax: (01232) 661 715.

Regional Arts Councils: see lists in handbooks, or telephone directories.

The Association of Authors' Agents, 37 Goldhawk Road, London W12 8QQ. Tel: (0181) 749 0315. Fax: (0181) 749 0318. The professional body which has code of practice.

Book Trust, Book House, 45 East Hill, London SW18 2QZ. Tel: (0181) 870 9055/8. Fax: (0181) 874 4790. Masses of information.

British Library Newspaper Library, Colindale Avenue, London NW9 5HE. Tel: (0171) 636 1544.

The Council for the Accreditation of Correspondence Colleges, 27 Marylebone Road, London NW1 5JS. Tel: (0171) 935 5391. Has lists of approved institutions.

Freelance Press Services, Cumberland House, Lissadel Street, Salford, Manchester M6 6GG. Tel: (01617) 458 850. Agents for the US *Writer's Digest* books.

Public Lending Right, Baytree House, Prince Regent Street, Stockton-on-Tees, Cleveland TS18 1DF. Tel: (01642) 604 6099. Fax: (01642) 615 641. All published books, all editions, should be registered and PLR money is distributed on the basis of library borrowings.

Shire Publications Ltd, Cromwell House, Church Street, Princes Risborough, Buckinghamshire HP27 9AA. Tel: (01884) 344 301. Fax: (01844) 347 080.

ADDRESSES IN DIRECTORIES

Check the prices before you send for them.

The Cottage Guide to Writers' Postal Workshops, Drakemyre Croft, Cairnorrie, Methlick, Ellon, Aberdeenshire AB41 0JN. Tel: (01651) 806 252.

List of Literature Festivals, The British Council, 10 Spring Gardens, London SW1A 2BN. Tel: (0171) 930 8466. Fax: (0171) 839 6347.

List of Literature and Creative Writing, Short Courses and Summer Schools in Britain, The British Council, 10 Spring Gardens, London SW1A 2BN. Tel: (0171) 930 8466. Fax: (0171) 839 6347.

Residential Short Courses, booklet published annually, £4.25, by The National Institute of Adult Continuing Education, England and Wales, 19b De Montfort Street, Leicester LE1 7GE. Tel: (01162) 551 451.

Directory of Writers' Circles, Jill Dick, Oldacre, Horderns Park Road, Chapel en le Frith, Derbyshire SK12 6SY. Price £4 – make cheques payable to Laurence Pollinger Limited.

Further Reading

The Author, The Society of Authors, 84 Drayton Gardens, London SW10 9SB. Tel: (0171) 373 6642. £6 per copy or £15 per year.

The Bookseller, J Whitaker & Sons Ltd, 12 Dyott Street, London WC1A 1DF. Tel: (0171) 836 8911. Fax: (071) 836 6381. £1.95 per copy or £108 a year. Main journal for the book trade.

Books for Keeps, The School Bookshop Association Ltd, Books for Keeps, 6 Brightfield Road, Lee, London SE12 8QF. Tel: (0181) 852 4953. £2.50 per copy or £15 per year. Review magazine of children's books.

The Woman Journalist, Barbara Haynes, 59 Grace Avenue, Maidstone, Kent ME16 0BS. Free to members of Society of Women Writers and Journalists. Articles of interest to professional writers.

Writers' Forum, John Benton, 9/10 Roberts Close, Moxley, Wednesbury, West Midlands WS10 8SS. Tel: (01902) 497 514. Subscription £14.50 per year.

Writing Magazine, Writers News Ltd, PO Box 4, Nairn, Scotland IV12 4HU. Tel: (01667) 454 441. Fax: (01667) 454 401. £1.80 per copy. 'How to' articles, competitions, market news, interviews and reviews.

Writers' Monthly, 29 Turnpike Lane, London N8 0EP. Tel: (0181) 342 8879. Fax: (0181) 347 8847. £33.50 per year. Information and advice for aspiring writers.

Writers News, Writers News Ltd, PO Box 4, Nairn, Scotland, IV12 4HU. Tel: (01667) 454 441. Fax: (01667) 454 401. Subscription £41.50 per year. Details of market opportunities, events, competitions, 'how to' articles, reviews and advice for writers.

PUBLISHERS OF REFERENCE BOOKS FOR WRITERS

Allison & Busby, 179 King's Cross Road, London WC1 9BZ. Tel: (0171) 833 1042. Fax: (0171) 833 1044.

BBC Books, Woodlands, 80 Wood Lane, London W12 0TT. Tel: (0181) 576 2000. Fax: (0181) 576 2858.

A & C Black (Publishers) Ltd, 35 Bedford Row, London WC1R 4JH. Tel: (0171) 242 0946. Fax: (0171) 831 8478.

Blueprint, Chapman & Hall Ltd, 2–6 Boundary Row, London SE1 8HN. Tel: (0171) 865 0066. Fax: (0171) 522 9623.

Robert Hale Ltd, Clerkenwell House, 45–47 Clerkenwell Green, London EC1R 0HT. Tel: (0171) 251 2661. Fax: (0171) 490 4958.

How To Books Ltd, Plymbridge House, Estover Road, Plymouth PL6 7PZ. Tel: (01752) 202301. Fax: (01752) 202331.

Hodder & Stoughton Educational, Teach Yourself, Hodder Headline plc, 338 Euston Road, London NW1 3BH. Tel: (0171) 873 6000. Fax: (0171) 873 6024.

Elm Tree, Hamish Hamilton, Penguin Books Ltd, Bath Road, Harmondsworth, Middlesex UB7 0DA. Tel: (0181) 899 4000. Fax: (0181) 899 4099.

Piatkus Books, 5 Windmill Street, London W1P 1HF. Tel: (0171) 631 0710. Fax: (0171) 436 7137.

William Heinemann, Reed Books, Michelin House, 81 Fulham Road, London SW3 6RB. Tel: (0171) 581 9393. Fax: (0171) 225 9424.

Routledge, 11 New Fetter Lane, London EC4P 4EE. Tel: (0171) 583 9855. Fax: (0171) 842 2298.

REFERENCE BOOKS – GENERAL ON WRITING AND PUBLISHING

Writers' and Artists' Yearbook, (A & C Black, £10.99). Lists publishers and magazines, plus gives advice on various aspects of writing and publishing.

The Writers' Handbook, Barry Turner (Macmillan Reference Book, £12.99). Another yearbook with lists and information.

The Author's Handbook, David Bolt (Piatkus Books).

Authors by Profession volume 2, Victor Bonham-Carter (Bodley Head). Volume 1 from the Society of Authors.

Inside Book Publishing: a career builder's guide, Giles N. Clark (Blueprint).

An Author's Guide to Publishing, Michael Legat (Robert Hale, £6.95).

Publishing and Bookselling in the Twentieth Century, F A Mumby (Unwin Hayman).

Willings Press Guide (Reed Information Services), Windsor Court, East Grinstead House, East Grinstead, West Sussex RH19 1XA.

Tel: (01342) 326 972. Fax: (01342) 327 100. Information about publishers/magazines, books etc.

DICTIONARY AND THESAURUS PUBLISHERS

There are hundreds to choose from, you can select one to suit your pocket and need. Most publishers produce large, concise, compact and pocket versions, hard and paperback. The major publishers are:

Cambridge University Press, The Edinburgh Building, Shaftsbury Road, Cambridge CB2 2RU. Tel: (01223) 312 393. Fax: (01223) 315 052.

Cassell plc, Wellington House, 125 Strand, London WC2R 0BB. Tel: (0171) 420 5555. Fax: (0171) 240 7261.

HarperCollins Publishers, 77–85 Fulham Palace Road, Hammersmith, London W6 8JB. Tel: (0181) 741 7070. Fax: (0181) 307 4440.

Helicon Publishing Ltd, 42 Hythe Bridge Street, Oxford OX1 2EP. Tel: (01865) 204 204. Fax: (01865) 204 205.

Larousse plc, Elsley House, 24–30 Great Titchfield Street, London W1P 7AD. Tel: (0171) 631 0878. Fax: (0171) 323 4694. And 43–45 Annandale Street, Edinburgh EH7 4AZ. Tel: (0131) 557 4571. Fax: (0131) 557 2936.

Longman Group Ltd, Longman House, Burnt Mill, Harlow, Essex CM20 2JE. Tel: (01279) 623 623/426 721. Fax: (01279) 431 059/ 451 946.

Oxford University Press, Walton Street, Oxford OX2 6DP. Tel: (01865) 56767. Fax: (01865) 56646.

ENCYCLOPAEDIAS

The publishers of encyclopaedias often publish concise or pocket editions as well as the larger versions.

The Cambridge Concise encyclopaedias (Cambridge University Press, £7.95, £17.85).

The Guinness encyclopaedias (Guinness Publishing Ltd, from £9.99 to £35.), 33 London Road, Enfield, Middlesex EN2 6DJ. Tel: (0181) 367 4567. Fax: (0181) 367 5912.

The Hutchinson encyclopaedias (Helicon Publishing Ltd, from £5.99 to £39.95).

The Macmillan encyclopaedias (Macmillan Reference Books £9.99

and £24.99), 25 Eccleston Place, London SW1W 9NF. Tel: (0171) 881 8000.

Pears Cyclopaedia (Pelham Books, Penguin, £14.99).

Wordsworth Encyclopaedia (Wordsworth Editions Ltd, £9.99), Cumberland House, Crib Street, Ware, Hertfordshire SG12 9ET.

OTHER REFERENCE BOOKS

This is just a selection, there are many more. Second-hand copies of the annual publications can often be obtained at a fraction of the cost of new editions, and may serve your purposes quite adequately.

Brewer's Concise Dictionary of Phrase and Fable (Helicon, £8.99).

Brewer's Dictionary of Names, People, Places and Things (Helicon).

Cambridge Biographical Encyclopaedia (Cambridge University Press, £29.95).

Chambers Biographical Dictionary (Larousse, £17.99).

Chambers Dictionary of Spelling (Larousse, £5.99).

Chambers Dictionary of Synonyms and Antonyms (Larousse, £4.99).

Collins What Happened When (Helicon, £4.99).

Collins English Spelling Dictionary (Helicon, £5.99)

Concise Dictionary of English Idioms B.A. Phythian (Hodder & Stoughton, £6.99).

Concise Dictionary of English Slang B.A. Phythian (Hodder & Stoughton, £6.99).

Concise Dictionary of New Words, B.A. Phythian (Hodder & Stoughton, £6.99).

Concise Dictionary of Phrase and Fable, B.A. Phythian (Hodder & Stoughton, £6.99).

Concise Oxford Dictionary of Proverbs (Oxford University Press, £5.99).

Egon Ronay's Cellnet Guide (Macmillan, £14.99).

Encyclopaedia of Dates and Events (Teach Yourself Books, Hodder & Stoughton).

Gascoigne Encyclopaedia of Britain (Macmillan, £29.95).

Good Hotel Guide Britain and Europe (Vermillion, £12.99).

Hutchinson Dictionary of Biography (Helicon, £12.99).

Hutchinson Pocket Fact Finder (Helicon, £7.99).

McNae's Essential Law for Journalists, Walter Greenwood (Butterworth & Co [Publishers] Ltd).

Oxford Dictionary of Modern Slang (Oxford University Press, £6.99).

Oxford Dictionary of Quotations (Oxford University Press).

Penguin Dictionary of Historical Slang, Eric Partridge (Penguin).
Penguin Dictionary for Writers and Editors (Penguin, £6.99).
Slang Down the Ages, Jonathon Green (Kyle Cathie, £16.99).
Whitaker's Almanack (J Whitaker & Sons Ltd).
Who Was Who in 9 volumes plus index (A & C Black).
Who's Who (A & C Black, 1995, £90).
Wordsworth Dictionary of Foreign Words in English, John Ayto (Wordsworth Editions Ltd, £2).

ATLASES

Major publishers of atlases, often in conjunction with other publishing houses, are:

AA Publishing
RAC
Philips
Ordnance Survey
A to Z

REFERENCE BOOKS ON PARTICULAR FORMS OF WRITING

Creative writing and general books

Becoming a Writer, Dorothea Brand (Papermac, £3.95).
The Complete Guide to Writing Fiction, Barnaby Conrad *et al* (Writer's Digest Books [USA], 1990).
Conflict, Action and Suspense, William Noble.
Getting into Print, Jenny Vaughan (Bedford Square Press, 1988, £4.95).
Get Writing, George Evans and Vince Powell (BBC Books, 1990, £4.99).
The Book Writer's Handbook, Gordon Wells (Allison & Busby, 1991, £6.99).
How to Get Published, Neil Wenborn (Hamlyn, 1990, £2.50).
How to Publish a Book, Robert Spicer (How To Books, £9.99).
How to Write for Publication, Chriss McCallum (How To Books, 1995, £8.99).
Is There a book Inside You?, Dan Poynter and Mandy Bingham (Exley, 1988, £6.95).
Research for Writers, Ann Hoffman (A & C Black, £10.99).
Revision, Kit Read (Robinson Writer's Workshop, 1991, £5.99).
Starting to Write, Marina Oliver and Deborah Oliver (How To

Books, 1996, £8.99).
The Successful Author's Handbook, Gordon Wells (Papermac, £7.99).
Successful Writing, George Ryley Scott (Lloyd Cole, 1993, £5.00).
Teach Yourself Creative Writing, Diane Doubtfire (Hodder & Stoughton, 1993, £5.99).
The Way to Write, John Fairfax (Elm Tree, £8.99).
Ways with Words: BBC Guide to Creative Writing (BBC Books, £8.99).
Word Power – A Guide to Creative Writing, Julian Birkett (A & C Black, £9.99).
Writers' Questions Answered, Gordon Wells (Allison & Busby, £6.99).
The Writer's Rights, Michael Legat (A & C Black, £8.99).
The Writing Business, Liz Taylor (Severn House, 1985, £3.95).
Writing for a Living, Ian Linton (Kogan Page, 1988, £8.99).
Writing for Pleasure and Profit, Michael Legat (Robert Hale, £4.95).
Writing Popular Fiction, Rona Randall (A & C Black, £7.99).
Writing Proposals and Synopses that Sell, André Jute (Writers News).
Writing Step by Step, Jean Saunders (Allison & Busby, £5.99).

Novels

The Art and Craft of Novel Writing, Oakley Hall (Story Press [USA] 1994, £9.99).
The Art of Romance Writing, Valerie Parv (Allen & Unwin, 1993, £7.99).
Bloody Murder, Julian Symons (Penguin, 1985, £3.95).
The Craft of Novel-Writing, Diane Doubtfire (Allison & Busby, £5.99).
The Craft of Writing Romance, Jean Saunders (Allison & Busby, £6.99).
Guide to Fiction Writing, Phyllis Whitney (Popular Press, 1984, £4.95).
How to Create Fictional Characters, Jean Saunders (Allison & Busby, £6.99).
How to Research Your Novel, Jean Saunders (Allison & Busby, £6.99).
How to Turn Your Holidays into Popular Fiction, Kate Nivison (Allison & Busby, £6.99).
How to Write a Blockbuster, Sarah Harrison (Allison & Busby, 1995, £7.99).
How to Write Crime Novels, Isobel Lambot (Allison & Busby, £6.99).
How to Write a Damn Good Novel, James N. Frey (Papermac, £6.99).
How to Write Historical Novels, Michael Legat (Allison & Busby, £5.99).

How to Write a Million, Dibell, Scott Card and Turco (Robinson Publishing Ltd, 1995, £9.99).

How to Write Novels, Paddy Kitchen (Elm Tree Books, 1981, £8.99).

How to Write Realistic Dialogue, Jean Saunders (Allison & Busby, £6.99).

How to Write Science Fiction, Bob Shaw (Alison & Busby, £6.99).

How to Write and Sell a Synopsis, Stella Whitelaw (Allison & Busby, £6.99).

How to Write and Sell Your First Novel, Oscar Collier with Frances Spatz Leighton (Writer's Digest Books, 1995, £9.95).

Plotting and Writing Suspense Fiction, Patricia Highsmith (Poplar Press, 1983, £4.95).

Writing Crime Fiction, H. R. F. Keating (A & C Black, 1987, £7.99).

Writing Erotic Fiction, Derek Parker (A & C Black, £8.99).

Writing Historical Fiction, Rhona Martin (A & C Black, 1995, £8.99).

Writing the Novel from Plot to Print, Lionel Block (Writer's Digest Books, 1979, £6.95).

Writing Science Fiction, Christopher Evans (A & C Black, 1988, £4.95).

Writing a Thriller, André Jute (A & C Black, £9.99).

Write a Successful Novel, Frederick F. and Moe Sherrard Smith (Escreet Publications, 1991, £7.95).

To Writers with Love, Mary Wibberley (Buchan & Enright, 1987, £4.95).

Use of English

Creative Writing, Mary Mackie (Gollancz, 1995, £8.99).

The Elements of Style, William Strunk Jr and E.B. White (Macmillan Publishing Co New York, £5.50).

Handbook for Written Language, Patricia Gordon (Hodder & Stoughton, 1995, £3.99).

The Nuts and Bolts of Writing, Michael Legat (Robert Hale, £4.95).

Punctuation Made Easy in One Hour, Graham King (Mandarin, £2.99).

Teach Yourself Correct English, B.A. Phythian (Hodder & Stoughton, £5.99).

Teach Yourself English Grammar, B.A. Phythian (Hodder & Stoughton, £5.99).

Write Tight, William Brohaugh (Writer's Digest, £10.85).

Index